The Good Granny
COMPANION

The Good Granny
COMPANION

Jane Fearnley-Whittingstall
Illustrated by Alex Fox

✳ SHORT BOOKS

First published in 2008 by
Short Books
3A Exmouth House
Pine Street
EC1R 0JH

10 9 8 7 6 5 4 3 2 1

A CIP catalogue record for this book is available from the British Library.

ISBN 978-1-906021-44-3

Printed in Great Britain by Clays

Every effort has been made to credit and obtain permission
for the material reproduced in the book. If any
errors have unwittingly occurred, we will be
happy to correct them in future editions.

CONTENTS

★ Introduction ★

'Grandmothers are all very strikt and they all sa
the same thing as they smile swetely over their gin
and orange. It is a grandmother's privilege to spoil
her grandchildren GET OFF THAT SOFA
NIGEL YOU WILL BRAKE IT.'
How to Be Topp by Nigel Molesworth (Geoffrey Willans)

For much of the time your grandchildren spend with you they will be happy doing what you do: cooking, cleaning (a toy Hoover has proved one of the most popular toys ever for toddlers), shopping. Having their 'help' may slow you down, but on balance it's more fun doing your chores with them than alone. To make their visit memorable, your trip to the supermarket could take in Story Time at the local library, or an open day at the Fire Station, or a pause beside a building site to watch diggers and cranes. You will have discovered, early on, the local playground, and saved up your stale crusts (the ones that make your hair curl) for the ducks on the canal.

But sooner or later, you will hear these words: 'Granny, I'm bored'; 'What can we do, Granny?'; 'Granny, can we make something?'; 'Granny why can't we watch telly?' There may also be times when you think, 'What on earth am I going to do with them for two whole days?' – or even two whole hours.

Here are the answers, all sorts of ideas and good advice collected from grandparents, and their children and grandchildren. As well as suggestions for outings, here are the rules of half-forgotten games, and instructions in half-remembered skills. An hour (sometimes less) spent showing your grandchildren how to play Patience and Beggar-my-Neighbour and how to sew, knit, bake a cake, or sow a packet of mustard and cress, is an hour well invested. Not only will you have spent a happy time bonding with them, you will also have earned half an hour to put your feet up and read your book, with a clear conscience, while they get on with their new-found skill.

The children, for their part, will have learned how to amuse themselves, a talent which will stand them in good stead in the long term, and for which their parents will be grateful to you. Moreover, you may yourself have renewed some forgotten skills and found that you enjoy them.

There will be other questions: 'Granny, who was the Greek god of war?'; 'When was the Spanish Armada?'; 'How long is an anaconda?'; 'What do hedgehogs eat?' We marvel at the thirst for knowledge that comes naturally to children, but we're often flummoxed by their questions. Help is at hand. Your *Companion* is ready with some of the answers, and guides you in the right direction for finding out the rest.

And there are times when you want to take your grandchildren somewhere special, as a birthday treat or just because you feel like it. The chapter on Great Days Out offers numerous inspiring alternatives, country-wide. If the outing is tailor-made for the child, it will be all the more successful, so there are suggestions for railway enthusiasts, wild life devotees, future farmers, and would-be knights and princesses, as well as the more usual theme parks and adventure playgrounds.

This book is intended, above all, as a source of good ideas to make it easy for you and your grandchildren to be interactive, and enjoy each other's company. It's all about having fun together.

♠ 1 ♠

Turn Off the Telly

'Granny, I'm bored. Why can't I watch telly?' Grandparents of my generation try not to reply, 'When I was your age we didn't have telly. We had to make our own amusements.' But we can't help thinking it. With a little help, our grandchildren can make their own amusements too, but only if we show them how much fun it can be.

Make 'board, not bored' your motto, and bring out the Chess, the Draughts (remember the game of Fox and Geese?) and the Backgammon. I looked after one grandson for a few days when he was just five, and every night we enjoyed a very grown up game of Dominoes. We played with a set of ebony pieces in a wooden box with a sliding lid. Beautiful, well-made equipment makes a game more pleasurable, so, if you are buying a Chess set, Dominoes, or even Snakes and Ladders, get the best you can afford. They will, with luck, last for generations. If the dog hadn't eaten two knights and a castle, I'd still be playing with the chess set my father taught us with.

These games, and Scrabble, are great to play when you have just one child to amuse. Lotto, Monopoly, and some of the card games described below, need three or more to be fun. They were all standard entertainment when we were children, but in many families have become marginalised. They definitely deserve to be revived.

FUN INDOORS

Sewing

Time and patience are needed when teaching children to sew and knit, and grandparents are more likely to be rich in these commodities than parents. Once your grandchildren have learned the basics there is much enjoyment to be had, with a little help from you, making dolls' clothes or Christmas presents. In our house a teddy has somehow survived since the 1970s, still wearing the same ill-fitting denim jeans and psychedelic tank top.

If you keep a rag bag, encourage the children to rummage through it. Those who have doubts about the pleasures of sewing may be converted by alluring scraps of silk, satin and velvet, ribbons, braid, buttons and sequins.

Tidying her sewing box was one of the enjoyable jobs my grandmother sometimes assigned to me. I delighted in the reels of silky cotton, the wooden darning mushroom, the sharp little scissors with ornamental handles, and some mysterious implements with hooks or loops on mother-of-pearl handles. Best of all was a long, flat, multi-stranded plait of brightly coloured mending threads.

With your help your grandchildren may, in due course, be capable of sewing on a button, fixing a fallen hem or replacing a broken zip. In case you have forgotten, here are instructions for the most basic stitches.

A STItCh In TIMe SaVEs nINe

RUNNING STITCH

Running stitch forms a broken line of stitches and is the most basic way to join two pieces of material. It's also useful for 'gathering', for example, to pull a full skirt in at the waist.

Thread the needle and knot the thread. Push the needle down through the material and then bring it back up to the side facing you, a little way in front. Repeat. Try to make short, even stitches, taking several of these 'running stitches' on to the needle at a time, before pulling it through the material. End with a backstitch to stop your stitches unravelling.

BACK STITCH

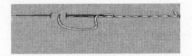

It makes a continuous line of stitches and is the strongest way to make a seam joining two pieces of material securely. Pull the needle and thread through the material from the back to the front. Insert the needle again, a millimetre or two behind the point where the thread came out. Pull the needle up through the material again, but this time the same distance in front of that point. Continue inserting and bringing up the needle half a stitch length behind and then in front of previous stitch.

OVERSEWING OR EDGING STITCH

Oversewing can be used as a decorative edging, or to join two pieces of non-fraying material together, such as felt.

Working from left to right, or vice versa, whatever is easier, push the needle down through the fabric and come back diagonally over the top. Space the stitches evenly, make them all the same length, and be careful not to pull them too tight.

Making and Dressing Paper Dolls

You will need:
Cardboard and card
Scraps of wool or doll's hair
Markers or crayons
Bits of Velcro
Scraps of material
Iron-on interfacing
Glue

This involves not so much sewing as cutting and sticking. But it is a good way of introducing a child to the fun of fabric and dress making. Draw a doll outline at least nine inches long or cut out a figure from a magazine, or download and enlarge a drawing from the Internet.

Paste the doll pattern on to cardboard and cut it out. Your grandchild can then make the doll into her very own by drawing in a face, and fingers, and gluing on hair.

Glue small pieces of Velcro on to the doll in the middle of the 'waist' and at the bottom of the 'neck'.

Make patterns for the doll's skirts, trousers and tops by pasting simple outline shapes on to card and then cutting them out.

Iron interfacing on to the back of the scraps of material. Then cut out the doll's clothes using the patterns and glue small pieces of Velcro on to the back of the clothing pieces to line up with the Velcro on the doll.

Making a Lavender Bag

Pick stems of lavender. Lay them out to dry on several layers of news-paper somewhere warm and dry like the airing cupboard. When completely dry, strip the flowers from the stems. Alternatively, you can buy dried lavender. You can make the bag out of cuttings or scraps of any clean material – old or new, the prettier the better – though cotton probably works best. Cut out 2 squares of material, not necessarily matching, with pinking shears or scissors. They should be about 6 x 6 inches. Draw a line in pencil or felt pen about $^1/_2$ inch in from the edge, all the way round. Stitch around three sides of the square in backstitch along this line. On the fourth side fold over a hem of about $^1/_2$ inch and sew. Next turn the whole bag inside out, so that the seams are inside and spoon in the lavender flowers. Then sew big running stitches across the open end in strong cotton, or embroidery silk, gathering it a little as you sew. Once you have gathered the top completely, tie the neck with a thin ribbon.

To Make a Sausage Dog

You will need:
Paper for making the pattern,
Felt – 1 large sheet approx 3ft/75cm sq for the body, and another smaller square approx 1ft/30cm sq for the ears and nose
Stuffing (you can either buy it, or use old tights, clean rags etc)
2 black buttons for the eyes

Good scissors – ideally pinking shears so that the seam edges,
   if you decide to leave them on the outside, will look more
   finished and won't fray
A marker pen to mark the sewing line
Needles and thread to stitch the dog together

Draw and cut out a pattern of a sausage dog from an old newspaper. Don't make it too small, as this will be harder to sew. Make the legs and tail thick and stumpy enough to give little fingers plenty of space to sew around and the whole dog can be reasonably 'cartoon' in style. Leave the ears until later.

Fold the large piece of felt in two. Pin the pattern to it and cut out. You now have the two sides of the dog, ready to sew together.

Mark with a pen lines all round the dog's outline half an inch in from the edge of the felt. This is to guide the sewers so they simply have to follow the lines, in back stitch or oversewing stitch (if you are not hiding the seams).

Sew everywhere except under the dog's tummy because that is where you will stuff it. You now have to decide whether to turn the dog inside out, before putting in the stuffing. This will mean that the seams are hidden and would look more professional. But young fingers may find it trickier
to sew and the dog will
still look very charm-
ing with the seams on
the outside.

Once the stuffing
is nicely balanced and
arranged right down

to the paws, sew up the 'tummy'. Sew a button on each side of the head to make his eyes and now, from the smaller piece of felt, cut out and sew on the ears and a small patch for the nose.

Knitting

Knitting isn't just a girly thing; on rainy days, my grandmother had my brothers as well as me knitting kettle holders and tea cosies with rug wool, on huge needles. My son was a keen knitter, too, for a while. Boys seem to be more ambitious, aiming for full sized Dr Who scarves rather than skimpy little numbers to drape round Barbie's neck. Indeed, Barbies are difficult to dress altogether; if only she would meet the same fate as Isadora Duncan, strangled when her floating scarf got caught in the wheels of an open car. Your grandson's Dr Who scarf is unlikely ever to get long enough to wear, so it's sensible to aim at something more manageable. If a scarf for a doll or Teddy is considered too babyish, a collar for the family pet might be just the thing.

I am assuming that most grannies will not have forgotten how to knit, but here is a reminder just in case. I learned to knit both plain and purl by muttering, 'In, over, through, off,' with each stitch and I found the mantra still worked when teaching my grandchildren. Your grandchild should sit down, and hold the needles in front of him, above his lap with the ball of wool on his lap. The bigger the needles and the thicker the wool, the quicker the progress. Even for a doll's scarf, size 8 needles and four ply wool are the minimum size for a beginner.

CASTING ON

Tie a small loop about six inches from the beginning of the wool and slip it over one of the pair of needles. Place this needle in the child's left hand. He then takes the other needle in the right hand and pokes its point into the loop on the left needle. Next he winds the wool over the top of the right-hand needle, so that it passes between the tips of the two needles

Now comes the difficult bit: the knitter carefully draws the right-hand needle a little way back towards him, picking up and catching the loop they have just made on the needle tip. He then takes that loop, and, without twisting it, slips it onto the tip of the needle in the left hand. Once he has managed this, a big pat on the back is due because he has just cast on his first proper knitting stitch.

Get him to cast on about ten stitches so that he can start to knit, in plain stitch, a doll's scarf.

PLAIN STITCH

The mantra for plain stitch is 'in', 'over' and 'through' exactly as in stage 2 of casting on. But instead of slipping the new stitch back onto the left hand needle, you catch it and keep it on the right-hand needle, then slip off the stitch you poked the needle into in the first place. When you have done this with all the stitches on the left-hand needle, so that it is empty, you can change hands and carry on until the doll's scarf is long enough.

PURL STITCH

Hold the needle that has the stitches on it in your left hand. Hold the other needle in your right hand. With the wool in front of the work, put the right-hand needle from back to front into the first stitch on the left-hand needle. The right-hand needle should be in front of the left-hand needle.

Form a loop by wrapping the yarn on top of and around the right-hand needle. Bring the right-hand needle under the left-hand needle and carefully pull the loop through the stitch with the right-hand needle to make a new purl stitch.

With the new stitch securely on the right-hand needle, slip the first or 'old' purl stitch over and off the tip of the left-hand needle.

CASTING OFF

Hold the needles with stitches on it in your left hand. Knit the first two stitches; insert the left needle into the stitch you knitted first, and pull it over the second stitch and completely off the needle. One stitch is now cast off. Knit one more stitch, again inserting the left needle into the first stitch on the right needle, and pulling it over the new stitch and off the needle. Repeat until one stitch remains. Now cut the wool from the ball, leaving a 6in end. Thread this end into a yarn needle and weave it into several stitches to secure it.

Tip: When the question 'But what else can I knit?' comes up, perhaps granny or grandpa would like a pair of wrist-warmers for Christmas. Simplicity itself – just two bands of straight knitting, not much wider or longer than the doll's scarf, each with the ends joined to form a bracelet loose enough for your hand to slip through.

Making Jewellery

Dried Pasta Necklaces

Tube-type pasta such as penne and macaroni
Embroidery threads, or string
Sellotape

This is a good, easy pastime for little ones. If you are using embroidery thread wrap the ends with sellotape to make it stiff. Then simply let the children thread the pasta on to the string and knot to make bracelets and necklaces. They can paint the pasta first, or glue glitter on to it.

A Simple Plaited Friendship Bracelet

Embroidery thread, in different colours
Masking tape or sellotape (any width)
Sharp scissors
Beads, for decoration, if you want

Cut three strands of different coloured embroidery thread about 15in/38cm long. Tie them together in a knot three inches from one end. Tape the top of the threads to a solid surface, using masking tape or sellotape. Separate the threads, and, using the thread on the left-hand side start plaiting by taking the left-hand thread over the middle thread and under the right-hand thread, and then bringing the right-hand thread back into the middle. Carry on plaiting until your bracelet is long enough to tie around your wrist, making sure you pull the threads tight each time you plait to give a firmer bracelet. Once it is long enough tie the ends in a knot so it doesn't unravel.

You can make a thicker bracelet by using six threads instead of three, still making three strands to plait, but each one this time being two threads thick. Plait in exactly the same way as before.

You can also thread and knot beads onto the ends of the ties.

To make it easier to thread small beads on to thick thread, put a little PVA glue onto the ends, squeeze it between your fingers to make a point and let it dry; or tightly bind tiny pieces of sticky tape around each end. When you have finished the bracelet the stiffened ends can be cut off.

A Button Necklace

Keep a button tin and let the children make a necklace or bracelet by threading small buttons, perhaps mixed with larger beads on to shirring elastic. This can be bought at any haberdashers and has the advantage of stretching to put on over a head or hand.

Bring the elastic back through the second hole in each button, to hold it firm on the necklace.

Tie it with a knot when it is long enough to stretch comfortably around the child's neck or wrist.

Great Card Games

We somehow learned to play traditional card games without being aware of being taught, usually at our grandparents' house, with granny and assorted cousins, uncles and aunts. It was an early life-lesson in the futility of arguing about rules, the shame of being a bad loser and the rare and ephemeral ecstasy of winning. The phrase 'It's not fair' was always howled down with derision.

Opinions are divided as to whether adults should allow children to win at games. My own instinct is that it's a grandparent's privilege to let the smallest ones win, but not every time. All too soon the boot will be on the other foot and they'll be wondering whether to let poor old granny win, when she fumbles her cards and can't remember what are trumps.

Simple as most of these games are, they are useful training for serious card playing in later life; knowing that spades, hearts, diamonds and clubs come in that order and an ace beats a king, gives you a head start at Bridge, Poker and Blackjack.

Snap

A good game for two, but more people can play. Packs of picture Snap cards, such as Animal Snap and even Maths Snap can be bought, and are fun for very small children, but the sooner they graduate to a proper pack of cards, the sooner you'll be able to call on them to make up a four for Bridge.

Shuffle and deal an equal number of cards to each player. Players must keep their cards face down in front of them.

Then they take it in turns to deal the top card from their pile into a central pile, looking at everyone's card to see if any matching cards are turned up.

When this happens shout, 'Snap'. The first person to say, 'Snap' gets all the cards in the centre pile. The game then continues until another person says 'Snap'. If a player says 'Snap' for no reason too many times, they are out. The game ends when one player holds all the cards.

Beggar My Neighbour (also known as Strip Jack Naked)

Another game for two or more. Shuffle and deal a standard pack of 52 cards. Each player holds his or her cards face down. The players take turns to turn over their top card and place it face up in the centre of the table, forming a pile. There are two kinds of card – the ace, king, queen and jack are picture cards, and the 2–10 are ordinary cards.

Play continues until a picture card appears. The player next in line to the person who played the picture card must give some cards to the central pile, depending on the value of the picture card. The payment rates are:

4 ordinary cards for an ace

3 ordinary cards for a king

2 ordinary cards for a queen

1 ordinary card for a jack

When the payment is complete (e.g. A has played a queen and B has put two ordinary cards on to the pile), the person who played the picture card (A in this case) takes the whole central pile and adds it to the bottom of his or her own pile.

If, while paying for a card, you turn over a picture card yourself, the previous deal is cancelled and the next person in the circle has to pay for the new picture card. The player who first runs out of cards loses.

The game can go on for a very long time.

Racing Demon

One of the great card games which children enjoy for years. It is very competitive. Granny may need to be on hand to prevent players coming to blows.

Any number can join in. Each player starts with a complete pack of cards (it's important that each pack has a different design or colour on the back, and small-sized Patience packs are ideal as they take up less space on the table or floor) and deals themselves a pile of 13, face down except for the top card, which is turned face up. This is called the 'tunnel'. They then deal themselves four more cards in a line face up next to their tunnel. The rest they keep in the hand.

At the word 'Go' the game starts: any player who has turned up an ace moves it into the middle and immediately replaces it from the top of their tunnel, turning the next card face up. Each player always has five cards face up: the card on top of their tunnel, and a line of four. There is no turn-taking: each player goes through their own remaining pack as quickly as possible, one, two or three at a time (you can agree on everyone doing the same at the beginning of the game, but one at a time is easier and quicker) building up the suits in the middle that have started with aces, and all the time watching for opportunities to move a card from their face-up line onto a middle pile. When putting cards in the middle they must always follow suit, so an ace of diamonds must be followed by a two of diamonds and so on. If someone else beats you with their two of diamonds then you must wait for someone to put out another ace of diamonds.

Cards from the face-up line are always replaced with the top card of their tunnel and the next card in the tunnel is turned up. The player who puts the final king onto a suit in the middle takes that pile and puts it to one side. This counts as five bonus points when adding up the score at the end of the game.

The winner is the first player to get rid of all their tunnel – not the four face-up cards as well: when they play their final card, putting it onto one of the suits in the middle, they say 'OUT' and play stops immediately.

Scoring is as follows: the winning player gets 10 bonus points. Any player who has claimed a suit with a king gets five bonus points.

All the finished suits claimed are now put back in the middle, face down, and the cards remaining in the middle are also turned over and sorted according to packs. Each player now collects his own cards from the middle and counts them up. Each card counts as one point. They must then subtract, as penalty points, the number of cards they have left in their tunnel to get their final score.

Old Maid

A good game for bringing a wide age range together. Let's not worry about the political correctness of the undesirable status of Old Maids!

Two or more players can play this game. Remove one queen leaving 51 cards. Deal all the cards and play from left to right. Some will have one more card than others – this does not matter. The players all look at their cards and discard any pairs they have.

The dealer begins by offering her cards spread face down to the player on her left. That player selects a card without seeing it, and adds it to her hand. If it makes a pair she discards the pair. She then offers her hand to the next player to her left, and so on.

If you get rid of all your cards you are safe – the turn passes to the next player and you take no further part. Eventually all the cards will have been discarded except one queen and the holder of this queen is the Old Maid, in other words, the loser.

Happy Families

The game has been popular since before the Great Exhibition of 1851. It was invented by John Jaques, also credited with inventing Tiddlywinks, Ludo and Snakes and Ladders (more essential contents of granny's games cupboard). A Happy Families pack consists of 44 – picturing the mother, father, son and daughter of each of eleven families. Each family has a trade or skill, for example, Mr Bun the Baker and Mr Bones the Butcher. Different versions are available, but the original designs, thought to be by Sir John Tenniel, are the ones grandparents prefer to play with, reminding us, as they do, of our own childhood. If you can't get hold of a pack, the game Go Fish, played with ordinary cards, is very similar.

All the cards are dealt, and players sort their 'hand' into families or parts of families. The player to the dealer's left begins. The player whose turn it is asks another player for a specific card: 'Have you got Miss Dip the Dyer's daughter,' for example, or 'Master Chip the Carpenter's son?' The asker must already hold at least one card of the same family.

If the player asked has the card it must be handed over and the asker continues by asking the same or another player for another card. If the asked player does not have the wanted card they say 'not at home' and the turn passes to them. Completed families are placed face down in front of the owner. When all families are complete, the player with most wins.

Patience

Patience, known in America as Solitaire, is a game played by one person. That means that, if you can enthuse your grandchild, you can give him a pack of cards, put your feet up and shut your eyes for half an hour or so.

There are lots of different Patience games – I give two here which are easy to learn and which I much enjoyed playing as a child. I used to play to make things happen, saying to myself, 'If this game comes out, it will be sunny tomorrow,' and much more private things, not to be divulged. The temptation to cheat was sometimes overwhelming.

Clock Patience

Shuffle and deal the full deck of cards, face down, into 13 piles of 4 cards each, laying them out in a circular 'clock' shape. You should have a pile of cards at each position from 1 o'clock to 12 o'clock and one at the centre. Go to the centre pile. Turn over the top card. See its value, which will be any number between 1 and 13, with aces being 1, jacks 11, queens 12 and kings 13.

Place the card you have turned over face up beside the pile that corresponds to its number on the clock. So. If you turn over a three, place it beside the pile in the 3 o'clock position. (Kings go in the centre.) Then turn over the top card from this pile. See its value and do the same as before. Do this as many times as possible. If you manage to reach a situation where no card remains face down, you have won the game.

Sevens

This is a another form of Patience, or Solitaire, which comprises seven vertical columns of cards, rather than a clock.

Deal out one card face up and place it at the beginning of an imaginary column on the left-hand side. Continue towards the right placing six more cards in a row next to each other, all face down.

Now, go to the second card in the row and place the next card from the deck face up on it. Continue placing a card face down in each of the cardpiles starting at the third card across the same way. Then, follow with the fourth card and so on, by placing a card face up on the first down card in the row and a card face down on each of the remaining piles of down cards. You will eventually have seven rows of cards laid out.

Hold the remaining deck of cards face down in your hand. Deal the first three cards off the top, and turn them over so you can see the third card in the deck. The object of the game is to use all of the cards in the deck by playing them. In order to play them, you must place each one on a pile of cards in alternative colours and in numerical order from the highest to the lowest – ie a red card on a black card, or a black card on a red card, and you must play a seven, for example, on an eight, or a jack on a queen. Any aces that are turned up are placed above the playing board to start new piles, and are built upon in suit from the lowest to the highest. An ace counts as one, so you need to play a two, three, four, etc, on the aces piles.

You can also move entire series of cards from one stack to the next. For example, if you have a pile of cards such as, red five, black four, red three, and black two, you can pick this pile up and place it on a pile that begins with a black six. Then, you turn the top card from the stack of cards that you just moved from, over, and continue to play on that one too, until there are no more cards left.

The game continues on until you cannot find any more moves to make. That means that the cards you have left in the deck cannot be played anywhere. On the other hand, if you can play the cards until they all end up on the aces, then you have won!

Pelmanism

A game with the very practical purpose of training the child's memory and keeping the grandparent's memory in better shape than it might otherwise be.

Shuffle the pack well and then spread all the cards face down and not touching on a table, a very big tray or the carpet.

The object is to collect identical pairs – two 3s, two kings, etc.

Players take it in turn to choose and turn over two cards, one at a time. However, unless they can make a matching pair, they must replace each card face down, in their original position, trying to memorise what cards they are and where they are. The winner is the one who collects the most pairs.

Whist

This is a game for 3 or 4 players, and an excellent introduction to the immortal game of Bridge. Whist shows the difference between suits, the principal of taking tricks and the way trumps work.

The dealer deals all the cards, placing the last card face up on the table. This is the trump suit.

The player to the left of the dealer starts the play and the others follow suit, playing from left to right. Before the dealer plays he takes the original trump card that he exposed.

If a player isn't able to follow suit he can play any other suit, including a trump.

The highest card in the suit that led wins the round (or trick), unless it is trumped, in which case the highest trump takes the trick. You then start the next round.

At the end, when all the cards in the hand have been played, you simply count the number of tricks won by each player.

Donkey

Play with 3 to 6 players. The aim is to avoid being 'donkey' i.e. last one out.

You play with the picture cards only and you must have four matching cards for each player. Thus a game with four players needs four kings, four queens, four jacks and four aces for play.

Shuffle and deal four cards face down to each player.

Then look at your cards and choose one card to get rid of. If you hold two or three of a kind, for example two queens, hang onto them and discard one of the other cards, where you hold only one card in the suit. Also before you get rid of any card decide what card value you want to collect.

Place your rejected card in front of the person to your left.

Pick up the card that has been placed in front of you by the player on your right. Keep it if it helps you, but get rid of another card on the next turn.

Once you have collected four of a kind put them down as quietly as possible. You are the winner. Don't let anyone know you have laid down your cards. The other players need to react by laying their cards down quickly, whether they have finished or not. The last person to lay their cards down is the Donkey.

All you Need is Paper and Pencil....

If you don't have a games cupboard full of board games, jigsaw puzzles and packs of cards with no cards missing, don't despair. Some excellent games only need a few sheets of paper torn from a note-pad, and a pencil or ballpoint pen for each player.

Consequences

A very entertaining old parlour game – definitely not just for Christmas. Best with four or more players. Each person needs a sheet of paper and a pencil. Everyone writes an adjective at the top of their sheet and carefully folds it over, so the next person can't see it. All players then pass their paper to their right-hand neighbour.

Everyone then writes at the top of the paper that has been passed to them 'the name of the man'. It might be someone they know (Uncle James), a famous person (Robbie Williams) or a fictional character (Horrid Henry). The paper is again folded down and passed on as before. Another adjective follows, then 'the name of the girl', followed by 'where they met'; 'what he said to her'; 'what she said to him'; then, 'the consequence was' and finally 'what the world said about it'. At every stage, before the papers are passed on, they must be folded down, so that what has been written is hidden. Once everyone has written 'what the world said', all the papers are collected and someone reads out the results, which can be hilarious, at least to anyone under the age of 12.

Here is an example:

Voluptuous Harry Potter met Vain Lucy Lockett on top of Everest.
He said to her, 'fasten your seatbelt.' She said to him 'I only drink
tea.' The consequence was, they ran the marathon, and the world said:
'How shocking.'

Battle Ships

A game for two players. Each player needs two pieces of paper. Each piece of paper is divided into squares – 10 squares across by 10 squares down. Each square is given a letter, A to J up the left side and 1 to 10 across the bottom. On one paper a player arranges their ships and records the shots of their opponent. On the other paper, they keep the score of their own shots.

To start the game, each player arranges a number of ships secretly on their squares.

Each ship occupies a number of consecutive squares on the grid, arranged either horizontally or vertically and depending on the ship's importance. An aircraft carrier occupies 5 squares, a battle ship 4 a destroyer and a submarine 3 each and a patrol boat 2. These are the standard type of ships in the game.

Only one ship at a time can occupy a square and both players must have the same number and types of ship. After the ships have been positioned each player has a turn. During his turn, the player names a list of target squares in the opponents' grid, which are to be shot at, for example D8.

If a ship occupies one of the squares, then it takes a hit. When all of the squares of a ship have been hit, the ship is sunk. After the target list has been given, the opponent then announces which of his ships have been hit. The round ends when all of one player's ships have been sunk.

The number of target squares that a player may shoot at in a turn is determined by the condition of the players' own ships at the beginning of the round.

Each player has as many shots as they have vessels afloat in each turn. So every time a player's ship is entirely destroyed, that player has one fewer shot on all subsequent turns.

Hangman

A simple game for 2 or 3. Players try to guess a word by filling in the blanks. Each wrong guess brings them closer to being 'hanged'.

One player chooses a word or phrase and marks a dash on a piece of paper for each letter of the word or words chosen. So the word 'dictionary', for example would have ten dashes.

Then they draw the 'gallows'. This looks like an upside-down 'L' with a short line, dropping down from its top end, for the 'noose'.

The other players must then guess the word, one letter at a time.

Every correct letter guessed is filled in on the appropriate dash. If it appears more than once in the word, it is filled in each time. So, if the guess was 'I', the 'dictionary' example would look like this:

$$\_\,I\,\_\_\,I\,\_\_\_\_\_$$

And each time the letter chosen is not in the word a body part is added to the drawing; starting with the head – a circle at the end of the 'noose' – and gradually adding the torso, the two legs, and the two arms.

If the whole 'hanged man' has been drawn before the word is guessed, the guessing player loses. The player who guesses the word or words first wins.

Squares (also known as Boxes)

This game has much in common with noughts and crosses, though it lasts longer and is not so weighted in favour of the player who goes first. On a piece of paper make a grid of dots. There can be any number, but 8 horizontal x 8 vertical is about right.

The players take turns to draw a line joining two dots. The aim is to make as many squares as you can, and to prevent your opponent making them. Every time you complete a square, you write your initial in it. When the whole grid has been filled in, the one with the most squares is the winner.

Drawing and Painting

There are obviously all sorts of ways to keep children occupied with drawing and painting – how creative you and the grandchildren get when you are together depends on your own inclinations and talents. A very good granny might encourage them to learn their letters and numbers by helping them make an 'alphabet book'. They can help you find a cardboard back and front cover for the book. Punch two

or three corresponding holes in each cover down one side and lace the covers together with string or ribbon, finishing in a neat bow at the front. Encourage the children to draw and paint and generally embellish the front cover, so it's their very own. Then they can put in, one at a time, pages of letters or numbers they have copied or drawings and paintings they have made.

If you are good on the computer, you can download pictures of favourite cartoon characters from the Internet to colour in. If you're more low-tech, give them old catalogues and magazines, scissors and PVA glue to cut out pictures and stick them into scrapbooks. When I was about ten, my pride and joy was my Royal Family Scrapbook, full of press cuttings of Princesses Elizabeth and Margaret Rose. Today's equivalent might be a scrapbook about a favourite TV or pop star – Daniel Radcliffe, or perhaps someone from *High School Musical*.

For art work in general, you can start a collage box, of small bits and pieces that you have hoarded for this very purpose – glittery sweet wrappers, old postcards and birthday cards, tinsel, old stamps, leaves, dried pasta, scraps of tissue paper – almost anything you can't bear to throw out. Children will love rummaging around in it, seeing form and beauty in the most unobvious things.

How to Make a Family Tree

Grandparents are in a unique position to pass on family history to their grandchildren. Stories about the wider family, going back several generations may be interesting, amusing or even sad and moving, and may be lost for ever when you are gone, unless you encourage the children to take an interest.

Making a family tree is a good way of doing this – an on-going project which you and they can add to bit by bit.

You will need:
A large sheet of paper or card
Pens in different colours
A notebook

Children can start by finding out about their own generation. Give them a notebook and get them to write in it their own names, which means all their first names and their surname and the same details for their brothers and sisters. Then they can write down everyone's date and place of birth. At the same time they can find photographs and collect family stories.

You can now help them collect a lot more information. They will need the full names, birth dates and birthplaces of both their parents: the full names, birth dates and birth places of their uncles and aunts, on both sides – their mother's family and their father's. They can then do the same for the children of their uncles and aunts – their first cousins.

Now, they need to collect the same information about you and their other three grandparents. After this they might find out about their grandparents' brothers and sisters, together with their husbands and wives – in other words, great uncles and great aunts. It is probably best to leave it at that, or the tree will become dauntingly complicated.

By this point there will probably be some dates and places of death and burial to include in the notebook. There may also be adoptions, divorces, perhaps, and even some interesting family skeletons for you, wise granny, to explain. At this stage you may think to yourself, no wonder entire organisations exist purely to chart the relationships and blood connections of families. It can all be quite confusing. So this is where you explain to the children that family trees make things easier to understand.

Show them an example of a family tree, to give them an idea of how it works and looks, before encouraging them to use all the information they have collected in their notebooks to plot their own. It needn't be solemn or stuffy; and it gives you, their granny, the opportunity to tell family stories and anecdotes as you chart the generations with them. The larger your piece of card, the more detail you can include on each person, though just the odd funny one-sentence description will enliven things considerably: e.g. 'Granny Mop (who made Mum walk about with a book on her head)'. It is a big project, to be spread over time.

Drawing the tree:

1.] Your grandchildren should write, in a line across the bottom, the names and details they have collected of themselves and all their first cousins. They should place themselves in the centre and plot the other names outwards on either side, putting their cousins via dad's family on one side and those via mum on the other. Distinguish between their own immediate family and the other cousins by choosing different colours of pen.

2.] They should then link each individual family by drawing 'a harness' – a parallel line – a little above each separate family of cousins, with short, vertical lines – 'stalks' or 'pointers'– leading down from it to each child in that family. They have now charted the current generation of the family.

3.] At this stage of the 'tree' it is best to plot things roughly, using

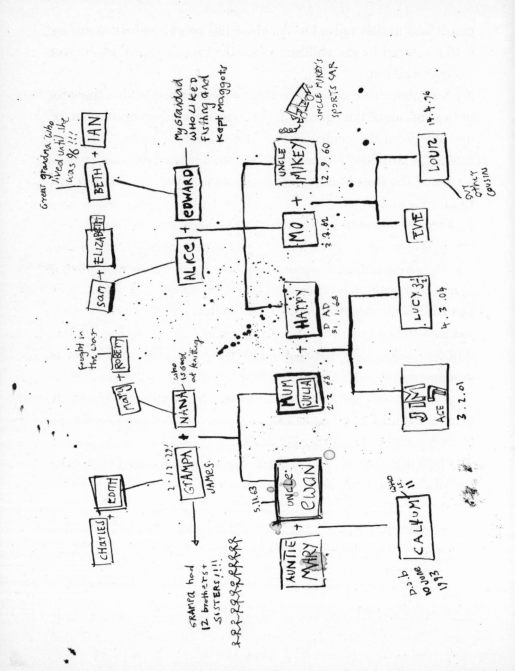

pencil and initials only; the details – full names and dates etc are better entered by the children when the proper spread of the tree has been laid out.

4.] Now they move up a row and back a generation to their parents, uncles and aunts. For each family of cousins they draw another 'stalk' upwards from the centre of the family 'harness' to the father and mother of that family. (Perhaps this is the point when you explain a bit about first and second cousins and even second cousins, once and twice removed.)

5.] This second row will consist of two family branches, their father's brothers and sisters and their mother's. Above these will come the two sets of grandparents . They must therefore draw a 'harness' linking their father and his brothers and sisters by a long stalk which leads up to the third row of the tree and reaches their father's mum and dad – one pair of their grandparents; then a similar 'harness' and 'stalks' (in a different colour) for their mother's family and the second set of grandparents.

6.] At this point you can help them decide whether they want to bring great uncles and aunts into the 'tree' and add more stalks and branches, and even another generation.

7.] Once they have plotted this they can add the details of birth dates and places – plus any pictures and details they can fit on – from the notebook.

8.] In the notebook, they can store all the extra details, photographs and so on, which they have collected and which would not 'fit' on the family tree.

Making a Map

You will need:
Crayons
One large piece of stiff white card
Scissors
Glue

Children love simple picture maps in books, whether they show the location of Dolly the carthorse's field in relation to the railway line, or the spot where the Pirates' treasure is buried.

Getting a child to make a map of where they live, as they see it, can be an engrossing project. This will be a map with the important things in life on it, and none of the boring stuff.

Encourage the child to think about the world around their home, what they like and don't like, and where they are in relation to each other. They are likely to note things like the local sweet shop, the nearest park – with swings and pond – and perhaps where their best friends' houses are. They can mark school, and the doctor, and the house with the whacky pink door up the road – whatever they want.

It doesn't matter whether things are in scale or not – school being a tiny building compared to the sweet shop is all part of the fun. For those who are not confident about drawing yet, teach them how to trace images from picture books or magazines.

Sometimes, rather than try to capture something in its entirety, you might encourage them to focus on the smaller details: you could, for example, get them to trace a horse chestnut leaf from a book on trees, to mark their favourite tree in the park; and perhaps a picture of a duck to show where they feed the birds in the park.

All you Need is Paper and Scissors....

These paper models came from a friend from the Netherlands, who made them again and again with her grandmother, or 'oma' (as the Dutch call their grannies). The patterns are very easy to follow, and have surprisingly effective results.

Paper Beads

These are made with strips of paper of different shapes, as shown overleaf in Fig 1. If you use coloured paper, you get surprising results, but don't use paper that is too thick.

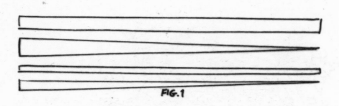

FIG.1

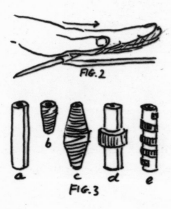

FIG.2

FIG.3

Fig 2 Roll a strip of paper round a thin knitting needle as shown. Stick the end down and remove the bead from the needle.

Fig 3. After you have made beads of different types and using different shapes of paper, you can put them on string and make a necklace.

Basket of flowers

For the flowers, the best thing to use is very colourful craft paper. You cut out a number of shapes and then stick them down to your own taste. This gives you a lovely example of a basket of flowers.

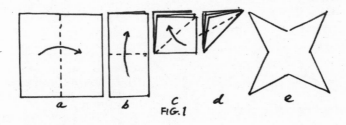

a   b   c   d   e

FIG. 1

Fig 1 Fold a square of paper as indicated at A B and C. Cut it, following the dotted line at D. When you open it up, you will see a star, as in E. You can cut a few stars all at once, by folding and cutting through several pieces of paper all at the same time.

Figs 2–7 Fold a square piece of paper as in A B and C of Fig 1. Cut it as shown in Figs 2–7, following the dotted lines. When you open them up, there will be different kinds of stars, crosses and flowers. Don't throw the offcuts away, because they can be used for when you make the flower basket. Now stick them down, as indicated here, in a basket – made from a folded piece of thick paper.

FIG.2

FIG.3

FIG.4

FIG.5

FIG.6

FIG.7

Sports plane

Fig 1 Take a thick square piece of paper, and fold it double with the fold at the top. cut out the body and the wings of the plane, as shown. The lines at A B C and D indicate notches that need to be cut.

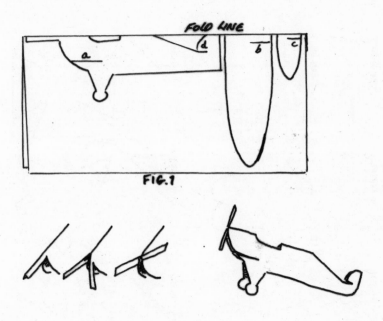

FIG.1

Fig 2 There is a protruding bit at the front of the body of the plane. Make it into a propellor by cutting and folding it (A B and C). After the propellor has been made, the plane looks like Fig 3.

Fig 4 The opened up big wing has to be slotted into the direction of the arrows. At C the wing and the body have been slotted together.

Fig 5 You can see the completed plane, after the tail wing has also been pushed into the slots.

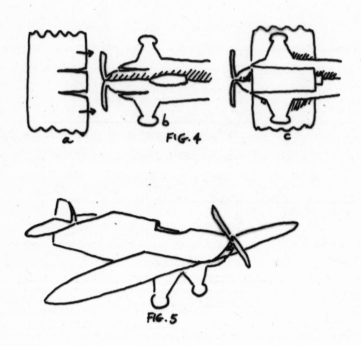

FIG. 4

FIG. 5

Playing with Dough

Children of all ages get satisfaction from kneading and squidging clay or dough and moulding it into useful or decorative shapes.

A free supply of genuine potter's clay may be more accessible than you think. If you are unlucky enough, as a gardener, to have areas of stiff soil too sticky to dig in winter and too dry and cracked to work in summer, you may be living on a vein of pure clay. It's easily recognised by its dense texture and putty-like colour. By sacrificing a small area of the garden, you can provide the ideal material for children to play Ancient Britons, digging up the clay to mould it into plates, bowls, cups and spoons, to be fired at a high temperature in granny's oven. Very good grannies may also grow a crop of woad for their Ancient Brits (*Isatis tinctoria* – it can be grown from seed).

More practically, you can buy readymade clay plasticine, which is non-toxic and does not dry out, so it can be used again and again. See Craftmill, Tel: 0161 4845888, E-mail: enquiries@craftmill.co.uk.

Less messy than plasticine or clay, play dough is very easy to make at home. Here is a simple recipe:

2 cups plain flour
1 cup salt
4 tablespoons of cream of tartar (sounds a lot but you do need this much)
2 cups water
2 tablespoons cooking oil (e.g. sunflower oil)
Food colouring

Mix the flour, salt and cream of tartar in a saucepan. Stir in the water, oil and colouring till the mixture is smooth.

Cook over a low heat for three to five minutes, stirring all the time. Remove from heat and set aside to cool. It is ready to use as soon as it is cool enough to handle. Don't worry if the mixture is a bit lumpy, it will become smooth as you knead it.

This will keep in a lidded plastic container for up to a year and can be brought out, rolled and cut into pieces to make any model that can be made with clay. Some suggestions are ladybirds, snakes, even the children's own hands and of course beads to thread on necklaces. These last can have holes for threading poked in them with cocktail sticks or drinking straws.

If they want to keep their efforts, you can bake them on a baking sheet for about 20 minutes (depending on their size). After they have been cooled on a wire tray, they can be painted using acrylic paint.

Granny's Toy Box

You could argue that you don't really need toys for small children as they have an amusing tendency to ignore them while making a bee-line for your keys, purse, mobile phone – indeed the entire contents of your handbag. Your necklaces and glasses make fascinating objects for babies to grab at too. (Rather than risk losing your keys down the back of a sofa, you may want to make up a special bunch of keys for baby from odd, unused ones lurking at the back of drawers.)

When young children visit you, they'll play happily with your saucepans, saucepan lids, sieves, wooden spoons and other safe kitchen stuff. But if they come fairly regularly or are left in your care, there are some toys worth investing in, to be kept at your house.

A **stroller**, full of wooden building bricks to push around and to empty and fill. I acquired the bricks when the first two grandchildren were about 18 months – now they are nine and still use them to build garages, castles, etc.

A **plastic lorry**, to transport the bricks.

Stacking cups or stacking rings, and a 'posting' toy.

A **rag book**, a **waterproof book** and a few floating toys for bath time.

A **soft ball** that makes electronic noises when rolled or thrown.

A **ball with a bell** inside it and a **rattle** or maracas give endless entertainment to very young children.

If you don't much care for garish plastic toys that play nursery rhymes (though children love them) a **wooden xylophone** is a more melodious alternative.

A **cheap toy cooker** with pots, plates and cutlery. This has proved popular in our house for several years.

Tip: These toys don't need to be new but can be perfectly good hand-me-downs, or bought from Oxfam or on ebay.

FUN AND GAMES OUTDOORS

Games for Two or Three

Ring-a-ring-a-roses

A popular game with tinies – you hold hands and dance round, singing the rhyme and collapsing together at the words 'we all fall down'.

Ring-a-ring-a-roses,
A pocket full of posies;
Atishoo! Atishoo!
We all fall down.

Hopscotch

Any number from one upwards can play – solitary children sometimes practise happily for hours (and it's very good exercise for granny).

Mark a grid (see illustration) with chalk on a hard surface, such as a paved patio or tarmac drive. The chalk will wash off. Number the boxes in the grid 1 to 10. The first player throws a small stone into square 1 and then hops through all the squares, one at a time, bending down to pick up the stone in square one on the way back. Next he throws the stone into square 2 and does the same thing and

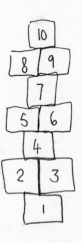

53

carries on until square 10 has been completed. A player is 'out' when she touches a line as she hops, or fails to pick up the stone.

The Matchbox Game

Give a child an empty matchbox and a list of small things to collect – a grey pebble, a petal, an empty snail shell and so on. If there is more than one child the first one back is the winner. Another way to play this is to give them a time limit – five minutes, say – to collect as many interesting things as they can.

Skipping Games

You will need a skipping rope, or a length of washing line. Teach them some skipping songs. Endless fun can be had, for example, 'running out' or 'running in' on their birthday month, keeping the rhythm going all the while.

> **All in together girls,**
> **This fine weather, girls.**
> **When it is your birthday**
> **Please jump out … January, February etc.**

Or simply performing actions while skipping to the rhyme:

> **Teddy bear, teddy bear touch the ground**
> **Teddy bear, teddy bear turn around**

Teddy bear, teddy bear show your shoe
Teddy bear, teddy bear that will do
Teddy bear, teddy bear go upstairs
Teddy bear, teddy bear say your prayers
Teddy bear, teddy bear turn off the light
Teddy bear, teddy bear say 'goodnight'.

Games for Family Get-togethers

Wheelbarrows

One child gets down on hands and knees and a second child picks him up from behind and holds him, by the legs, so he is walking on his hands. Four children or more can make enough 'wheelbarrows' to have a race.

The Obstacle Game

Set out a number of 'obstacles' in the garden – some possibilities:

A bucket and tennis ball
A skipping rope
Some serving spoons and small potatoes
Some black plastic sacks
A sturdy chair to climb over

The children can be timed by you as they cover this course, one at a time. They must throw the ball twice into the bucket standing behind a line, then run on to complete a set number of skips with the skipping rope, next on to the spoons, where they must carry a potato balanced on a spoon for a set distance, then climb into a bin liner and jump another set distance, climb on and over the garden chair and run for 'home'.

You can make endless variations of your own. Remember to set handicaps to give younger children a chance.

Grandmother's Footsteps

This one is for you! Turn your back to the children who must all stand an agreed distance away from you. The aim of the game for them is to be the first one to sneak up on you without being seen. You can catch them out by suddenly turning round and, if they haven't managed to 'freeze' before you see them, they must go back to the starting line and begin again.

'What's the Time, Mr Wolf?'

One child or adult is chosen to be Mr Wolf. The others start behind a line some distance away and try to sneak up on him. They call out 'What's the time, Mr Wolf?' and he, with his back turned, replies: 'One o'clock!' They then try to get closer, calling out; again, 'What's the time, Mr Wolf?' Mr Wolf replies, 'Half past three!' He does not turn around until he senses someone is getting very close to him.

Then he turns and cries in a terrible wolf voice 'Dinner time!' Everyone takes flight, squealing as they go and Mr Wolf tries to catch as many as he can for dinner.

O'Grady Says, or Simon Says

One child is O'Grady or Simon and stands facing the others. He performs a number of different actions, waving his right arm, hopping on his left foot, winking and so on, The others must do as he says, but only if prefaces his commands with O'Grady, as in 'O'Grady says, "do this". If he says only 'Do this,' any player who still obeys him is out. The trick is to lull the children into forgetfulness by issuing lots of 'O' Grady says' and then suddenly sneaking in a 'Do This.'

Statues

One child turns her back and the others run around behind her, keeping a wary eye on her in case she turns around suddenly, when they must all freeze into the position they are in when she turns. A statue caught moving is out.

Blind Man's Buff

Blindfold the 'blind man' with a thick scarf. Turn him round a few times and then set him off to catch the other children who will be dancing around the blind man. The winner is the blind man who catches the most, or the player who is caught last.

Shoeing the Horse

You will need a blindfold, four plastic cups – the cups from giant detergent packets are ideal and a four-legged chair with legs that are thin enough to fit into the cups. Blindfold the children in turn, spin them around and take them to the chair, where you have arranged the cups around the legs at random. They must feel for a cup and try to put a leg into it. When they have succeeded, they must try with the next cup, until they have put four 'shoes' on the 'horse'.

Pin the Tail on the Donkey

Draw on a piece of card a large cartoon donkey shape at least two feet by one and a half, but minus a tail. Attach it to a wall at child level. Blindfold the children one at a time and hand them 'the tail', which can be an old tie with a drawing pin, or a cardboard tail with blu-tack on it that you have drawn and cut out. Then lead them to the donkey and ask them to stick the tail in the right place. This can be very funny for childish spectators.

Crazy Golf

You need a ball and something to hit it with – an old tennis racket, a cricket bat or a putter, and some things to construct some very basic obstacles. A couple of flowerpots to aim between, with a third on its side to aim into as the final hole. You can make a simple cardboard box tunnel and construct a makeshift ramp out of a brick with a piece of wood running up on to it. The child who completes the course using the fewest strokes in the fastest time is judged the winner.

French Cricket

One child holds a racket or bat while another, the bowler, throws a tennis ball at him, trying to hit below the knee, and the rest field in a circle round him. If the batsman manages to hit the ball back, he is allowed to turn in the direction of the next ball to defend himself. If he fails then he must remain as he is and defend himself without turning his body in the direction of the ball. If the batsman falls over, or if the bowler manages to hit him below the knee, he is out, in which case he becomes a fielder and someone else takes his place. A batsman can also be caught out. Otherwise children can simply take turns at batting and bowling. This is great fun when played on a beach.

Pig in the Middle

A child stands in the middle as the pig, while two others throw a tennis ball backwards and forwards over her head to each other. When the pig manages to catch it, the thrower becomes 'piggy'.

On the Beach, in the Country....

Ducks and Drakes

My brothers used to spend happy hours playing Ducks and Drakes on the beach, beside a river or pond, anywhere where there is a reasonably calm stretch of water. I was useless at it but I still haven't given up trying.

First, find suitable flat, smooth stones on the beach and then show the children how to send them skimming and bouncing across the water by throwing them with a special flick of the wrist. For those who must compete, the one who gets the most bounces with a single pebble wins.

Scavenger Hunts

Organise a scavenger hunt on the beach. List a number of things for the children to find and bring back to you.

Lifeboats and High Water Marks

Many seaside towns or villages have open days when you can learn all about the work of the lifeboat service, but you don't have to wait for a formal occasion to get grandchildren interested. The Grace Darling story (on page 235) is a good one to tell.

Children are interested to learn that lifeboats are manned by ordinary people, not special sailors. If the maroon signal is heard it's often the butcher, the baker or builder who will make that dramatic dash to the boat, risking their lives to go out and save people who are in trouble at sea.

If you are in an area where there has been flooding, encourage children to look out for the high water mark signs which are sometimes etched onto walls. It's sometimes amazing how high the floodwaters have risen.

An Echo Hunt

Children who protest at the idea of 'Going for a walk' in the country are not so prone to drag their heels if you have an interesting goal in mind. As children, we were fascinated by places with echoes. There was a particular valley we walked in which had a wonderful echo. We would spend hours calling to it and waiting for the 'reply' to come echoing back. There was also a viaduct we walked under which had an equally impressive but slightly eerier echo.

Sadly in an over-crowded island there are fewer echoes nowadays. But you may know a steep-sided valley with few trees to absorb the sound where you can take your grandchildren to test the echo with their shouts. They may like to hear the story of 'Echo and Narcissus':

Echo was a beautiful nymph who loved talking, had a quick wit and liked the last word. One day the goddess, Hera, suspecting that her husband was playing and flirting with the nymph behind her back, set out to look for him. Echo angered Hera, by keeping her talking and so giving her husband time to escape. Hera swore in revenge that Echo would lose the use of her tongue except for the purpose of reply.

'You shall still have the last word,' said Hera, 'but no power to speak first.'

Some time later, Echo fell in love with a beautiful boy, called Narcissus, when she saw him one day out hunting with his friends in the woods. But, because of Hera's curse, she could not speak first.

Before long, Narcissus became separated from his friends, and called out, 'Who's here?'

Echo replied, 'Here.'

Narcissus looked around, but seeing no one called out, 'Come.'

Echo answered, 'Come.'

As no one came, Narcissus called again, 'Why do you avoid me?'

Echo asked the same question.

'Let us join one another,' said Narcissus. And Echo answered in the same words and ran to meet him.

But poor Echo was spurned by Narcissus. She wasted away in despair, until finally all that was left of her was her echoing voice.

Looking at Tombstones

Here lies the body of Paddy Smith,
An Irishman entirely,
He bought his tombstone second hand
His name's not Smith, it's Riley.

You won't find this inscription on a tombstone. It's just a joke that the Irish mother of a friend liked to recite. In a country village, you might consider taking the children – respectfully, of course – into the churchyard to admire the church and to look at the tombstones; some of the more ancient gravestones will have inscriptions engraved on them that will intrigue older children.

Encourage them to look at the dates and names engraved on church lintels and walls and to look for symbols and creatures on plaques and head stones. Can they find a carved lion – a symbol of good – or a frog, which represents a sinner? Point out any gargoyles and grotesques, high up on the building; they may be relieved to learn that the gargoyles are really just imaginative waterspouts.

Animals – Where They Live and What They Eat

Most children are intrigued by wild animals and will enjoy finding out more about them, speculating about which animal lives in which hole, looking for scraps of fur on barbed wire fences, and spotting different paw prints and droppings. They probably already know Fantastic Mr Fox from Roald Dahl's book, and, if granny has had her say, the Squirrel, the Hare and the Little Grey Rabbit from Alison Uttley's series of stories, so much loved by my generation. If you include in your grandchildren's reading list *The Wind in the Willows* and the complete works of Beatrix Potter, they will start with a pretty extensive knowledge of British wild life, and will know what to look for.

Badgers

[Badger] shuffled on in front of them, carrying the light,
and they followed him... down a long, gloomy, and,
to tell the truth, decidedly shabby passage, into a sort of
central hall; out of which they could dimly see other long
tunnel-like passages branching, passages mysterious and
without apparent end.

The Wind in the Willows by Kenneth Grahame

'Our' badger, and Kenneth Grahame's, is the Eurasian badger, found not just in Britain and Ireland but in mainland Europe, Asia and Japan. These badgers eat worms (up to 200 in a night), also slugs, frogs, seeds, berries, mice, and even baby rabbits. Wasps' nests are a particular delicacy on a badger's menu. If only they would restrict their diet to slugs, they'd be most welcome in my garden.

Badgers live in underground setts which they build in places ranging from ancient woodlands to recently developed housing estates. They prefer areas where it is easy to find food and there is enough cover to raise their cubs with the minimum of disturbance.

Foxes

John, John, the grey goose has gone
And the fox has gone to his den-Oh.
Anon

Foxes are found in woodland and open country, but their presence in urban and built-up areas is increasing. They tend to live in families, each family defending its territory which, in the country, can be anything from 25 to 5000 acres. Urban foxes cover much smaller areas, usually near a good source of food. Foxes usually shelter and breed below ground in an 'earth' or 'den'. They prefer well-drained soil, and will often use the burrows previously left by rabbits or badgers. Urban foxes tend to live beneath sheds and outbuildings, and have even been known to live under the floorboards of houses.

Foxes are not choosy eaters and will devour small mammals, birds (including their eggs), reptiles, insects, earthworms, fruits and vegetables. As countless stories tell, farmers endlessly wage war on foxes, trying to protect their hens, geese and ducks, but in most tales, the cunning fox outwits the farmer. Urban foxes have become particularly good at scavenging for food in waste bins and bags, and will sometimes fight small pets for scraps of pet food.

Stoats and Weasels

Q. *How do you tell the difference between a weasel and a stoat?*
A. *A weasel is weasily distinguished, but a stoat is stoatally different.*

Stoats live in woodland and are strictly meat eaters. They hunt for live prey and don't scavenge like foxes. They mainly eat small rodents such as voles and mice. But stoats – which are larger than weasels – will also eat hares, rabbits and birds.

Dormice

'The Dormouse is asleep again,' said the Hatter, and he poured a little hot tea upon its nose. The Dormouse shook its head impatiently, and said, without opening its eyes, 'Of course, of course; just what I was going to remark myself.'
Alice's Adventures in Wonderland by Lewis Carroll

Dormice live in woodlands and hedgerows, particularly where there are oak and hazel and sweet chestnut trees because they feed on the nuts. In the spring they eat flowers, such as honeysuckle and pollen. Fruit, nuts and berries and small insects are their autumn diet. In the winter dormice hibernate in nests under the leaf litter on the forest floor. When they wake in spring, they build woven nests of honeysuckle bark and fresh leaves in the undergrowth. If the weather is cold and wet, and food scarce, they save energy by curling up into a ball and going to sleep. They are tiny (8–9cm), with an equally long tail, and shy and are a protected species because they are becoming rare. They are only found in the south of England.

Squirrels

This is a Tale about a tail — a tail that belonged to a little red squirrel, and his name was Nutkin. He had a brother called Twinkleberry, and a great many cousins;
they lived in a wood at the edge of a lake.
Squirrel Nutkin by Beatrix Potter

The commonest squirrels in this country are the hardier grey squirrels; they have largely driven out the red squirrel which is less adaptable.

Grey squirrels live mostly in woods, as trees provide plenty of food and shelter. They prefer old woods with a mixture of trees, good ground cover, and bulbs, fungi and berry-bearing bushes. Good food trees for grey squirrels include Oak, Hazel, Ash, Field Maple, Sycamore, Hornbeam and Sweet Chestnut. Grey squirrels can adapt to the open and can be seen flying up and down trees in parks and gardens. Home for a squirrel is either a nest called a drey, hidden in the high branches, or a den in a hollow tree. They will also live in

lofts and eaves when roofs have holes in them. They eat catkins, flowers, rose hips, shoots and bark. They sometimes rob nests in spring, taking both eggs and young birds. However, their most important natural food is tree seed and nuts. They store these under the earth in 'caches', each with only a couple of nuts or seeds. They sniff these out when food is short in winter. The problem is that grey squirrels damage trees — foresters refer to them as rats with fluffy tails.

Cuckoos

O Cuckoo, shall I call thee 'bird' or but a wandering voice?
State the alternative preferred, with reasons for your choice.
Parody of **'To the Cuckoo' by William Wordsworth**

Cuckoos arrive from Africa in the spring; the females come first and the males, who make the famous cuckoo call, follow them. There is always competition to hear the first cuckoo call, but there are fewer cuckoos today, and the species is now protected.

The cuckoo, a large bird, lays its eggs in other, smaller birds' nests, leaving its young for the other bird family to rear. When the young cuckoo hatches, almost the first thing it does is to push all other fledglings out of the nest, so keeping all the food for itself! As soon as it has learnt to fly it follows its parents back to Africa.

In April the cuckoo comes,
In May he sings.
In June changes his tune,
In July gets ready to fly
In August go he must.

Hedgehogs

Fuzzypeg is a young hedgehog who appears in Alison Uttley's *Little Grey Rabbit* stories, and Mrs Tiggywinkle is the 'very stout, short' heroine of one of Beatrix Potter's much loved stories.

Most hedgehogs are night creatures, although some kinds are more likely to come out in the daytime. Hedgehogs use their snouts to dig out a den for shelter. They sleep for much of the day either under cover of a hedge, bush or rock or in a hole in the ground. In gardens they sometimes shelter in wood piles. They hibernate in winter, waking as the weather gets warmer. When frightened they roll themselves up into a ball of spines.

Hedgehogs are considered good for gardens as they feed on insects and snails, and if there was a hedgehog in the garden, people used to encourage it by putting out a saucer of bread and milk. In fact, this is not a good idea as it upsets their little tummies. Slugs and snails are not good for them either; they only turn to these when desperate.

The hedgehog's ideal diet consists of beetles and caterpillars, and sometimes earthworms. Don't be tempted to make a pet of a hedgehog. Because their prickles prevent them grooming themselves, they are infested with fleas and ticks.

Moles

Don't make a mountain out of a molehill

In 1702, when William of Orange's horse tripped over a molehill and fell, causing the king's death, his enemies the Jacobites used to raise their glasses to toast 'the little gentleman in black velvet'.

You never see a live mole and seldom a dead one, as they live almost entirely underground. They have small cylindrical bodies, covered in soft fur of a grey-black-brown non-colour described as taupe, which is French for mole. Their eyes are so tiny that they are virtually blind. Their diet consists mainly of earthworms, but they occasionally dine on small mice that stray too close to their burrows.

Moles paralyse worms with a poison in their saliva and then store them, still living, in underground larders until they are hungry. As they make their underground burrows, they throw up annoying mounds of earth, known as molehills, all over granny's lawn. If you put the molehill soil into trays or flower pots, it makes good seed compost.

Recommended source of information about native animals and farm animals: *Fauna Britannica* **by Duff Hart Davis**

Flowers

If you love flowers, you'll want your grandchildren to share your interest and your knowledge. You can start, on country walks, by picking a buttercup and holding it under their chins to see if they like butter, showing them how to tell the time with a dandelion clock and doing 'loves me, loves me not', with the petals of a moon daisy.

Make a ballerina from a poppy, turning down the petals and fastening a piece of stem around the waist.

Teach them to suck the nectar from a honeysuckle flower, to chew a juicy grass stem or a wild sorrel leaf, and to rub a dock leaf on a nettle sting to soothe it.

My brother used to pick a long blade of grass, hold it between his thumbs, and blow on it to make a screeching sound. I tried and tried, but only occasionally got the hang of it. He could also hoot like an owl by blowing through his closed fists, another art I never mastered.

If you have these skills, pass them on to a new generation. In the garden, demonstrate how snapdragon flowers can 'bite' little fingers; put a foxglove on each finger tip; show them how to dead-head tulips and irises by snapping off the stems just below the spent flowers.

We used to spend happy hours looking for a lucky four-leaved clover in granny's lawn. Nowadays clover tends to get weed-killed out of lawns, but if yours is not a perfect bowling green, encourage the children to search – it gives granny a chance to make a cup of tea and sit down for a bit.

When autumn comes, take the children to pick blackberries and mushrooms and show them hips and haws and hazel nuts in the hedgerows. Help them make an album of autumn leaves, writing the name of the tree by each leaf.

Pressing flowers and leaves

Collect flowers when they are dry but before the sun has wilted them. Pansies press well but you can use most flowers, although those with thorny stems are best avoided.

Flatten the flowers carefully, using your finger; if the centre is very dense you can remove some inside petals. Press a few leaves at the same time, to have a record of the whole plant. Use a big, heavy book and place the flowers inside it, between two sheets of paper. We used to use blotting paper, but nobody has it any more. Any plain white paper can be used, the more absorbent the better. The flowers must not touch each other. Pile more books on top and leave the flowers to dry for two weeks. When they are completely dry the children can place them in a scrapbook or a special book they have made, writing in the name of the flower and the time and place they picked it.

Leaves can be dried in the same way but their colour may not last. Before pressing leaves, make sure they are dry and flat. Place the leaves to be pressed between two sheets of newspaper. Put some heavy books on top of them. Allow them to flatten and dry like this for at least 24 hours. When they are dry, look in a book of trees with your grandchildren and help them recognise the name of the leaf by its shape.

Making a daisy chain

Daisy, Daisy, give me your answer do,
I'm half crazy all for the love of you.
It won't be a stylish marriage, I can't afford a carriage.
But you'll look sweet upon the seat of a bicycle made for two.

Harry Dacre 1892

Very small children love to wear daisy chains as jewellery, and older ones enjoy making them. I remember attempting the longest daisy chain ever with my brother, in the hope of getting into the *Guinness Book of Records*. It kept us occupied for days and stretched from one end of our grandparents' lawn to the other twice over before rain stopped play.

Pick the daisies as close to the ground as possible so that there is a long enough stem to work on, and choose those with the thickest stems. Using your thumbnail, carefully splice a slit in the stem towards the end. Pull the stem of a second daisy through the slit so that its stem is sticking out. Then slit this stem and thread a third daisy through that. Continue like this until you have enough for a bracelet, a necklace or a crown.

Recommended source of facts and folklore about plants: *Flora Britannica* **by Richard Mabey.**

◆2◆

Seasonal Fun

Children look forward to the main festivals of the year with mounting excitement as the dates draw near. It's important to them that the celebratory rituals remain more or less unchanged from year to year. And for us, it's reassuring if they remain unchanged from generation to generation. It is, naturally, grandparents who can make sure that this is what happens.

EASTER

Easter is the time when Christians celebrate the resurrection of Jesus, and, Christian or not, we all give each other decorated eggs, usually, nowadays, made of chocolate. But the custom of decorating eggs goes back far earlier. The ancient Persians painted eggs for Navrooz, their New Year celebration, which falls on the Spring equinox, a tradition that is at least 2,500 years old. Sculptures on the walls of Persepolis show people carrying eggs for Navrooz to the king.

In the Christian tradition, eggs symbolise rebirth. For Orthodox Christians, Easter eggs are dyed red to represent the blood of Christ, and the hard shell of the egg symbolises Christ's sealed Tomb. In Orthodox and Eastern Catholic churches, Easter eggs are blessed by the priest and distributed to the faithful.

For us, the Easter Bunny (originally a hare) brings the eggs and hides them for children to find. In the North of England, a traditional game is played at Easter, where hard boiled eggs are distributed and each player hits the other player's egg with their own – like a festive game of conkers. This is known as 'egg tapping', 'egg dumping' or 'egg jarping'. The winner is the holder of the last intact egg. In Scotland and north east England painted hard-boiled eggs are traditionally rolled down steep hills on Easter Sunday.

Tip: Parents will be grateful if, instead of adding to the avalanche of chocolate, you give your grandchildren small Easter presents. You can buy pretty cardboard or tin eggs to put them in. Or give each child a prettily painted wooden egg each year, so that gradually they build up a collection. Look for them in shops selling handicrafts.

An Easter Egg Treasure Hunt

For under-fives a simple Easter Egg Hunt is easy to organise indoors or out. The Easter Bunny, disguised as granny, hides the eggs before the children arrive, or while they're having lunch. To make sure each child gets his share, hide the eggs in 'nests', with the same number of eggs in each nest as there are children. The rule is that each child may take one egg from each nest. There can be an extra prize for the one to find all the nests first.

For a more sophisticated variation, you could organise a Treasure Hunt with clues.

You need no more than eight clues. For younger children the clues should simply be 'directions'. Each clue should be the name of a something familiar, easy to reach and safe, inside the house or, depending on the weather, in the garden.

Some clues:
Behind the kitchen door (starter clue)
1. **Next to the bath**
2. **Under the sofa**
3. **Next to the fridge**
4. **Under rug in the hall**
5. **In the laundry basket**
6. **Behind the curtain**
7. **Under the hall table**

For very young children who cannot read, drawings of the 'clues' might help them to join in.

One of the ways of making the hunt fair is to have each child bring back a 'tell' from the site of each clue: write or draw each clue on a separate piece of brightly coloured paper or card – Post-It notes are ideal for this. Then, depending on the number of children – in this example 4, write (or ask the children to write) on separate pieces of paper, the number '1' four times, number '2' four times, and so on, up to the total number of clues. Now, keeping back the starter clue, hide the other seven clues putting the four number '1's alongside clue number one, the four '2's with clue number two and so on.

Read the starter clue to the assembled children, who must then follow it and find the next clue. In this example they would go to the kitchen door, where they would find clue 1 and also the four written 'number 1s'.

Before rushing on to the next clue, each child must bring you back the number of the clue they have found. They must do this with each clue to ensure that no one rushes straight to the end and misses the fun of the hunt. At the final clue (under the hall table) there can be a small Easter egg for each child. There could be a 'champ's' prize to the child who finishes first.

If you do the treasure hunt in the garden, put the numbers in egg cartons, yoghurt pots or small containers so that they won't blow away and put the clues in plastic eggs, or write them on small pieces of wood with marker pen and keep them for future treasure hunts.

For older children you can write the hiding place clues as riddles.

Examples:
I'm a little _____ short and stout etc...
(for an egg hidden in a teapot)

Hickory, dickory, dock
The mouse ran up the_____ (an egg near the clock)

Old Mother Hubbard lived in a _____

Humpty Dumpty sat on the _____

Scratch your nose and shake your head
The next clue is under the _____

Don't be cross, no need to frown
Look under a place where you sit down

Follow this clue to a very cold place
Where lots of ice cubes take up the space

Roses are red, lavender's blue
Look in the flowerbed for your next clue

Curl up small, if you are able
Because the next clue is under the _____

Turn around and touch the floor
The next clue is behind the _____

Out in the garden where the birds sing and perch
Next to the lawnmower/shed/swings is the best place to search

The sun has put his _____ on (under a hat)

You can also simply have a single letter to be found with each clue, which the children have to collect to form an anagram and then unscramble at the end, to work out the hiding place of the treasure.

A Very Simple Easter Bonnet

In your Easter bonnet, with all the frills upon it,
You'll be the grandest lady in the Easter Parade.
I'll be all in clover and when they look you over,
I'll be the proudest fellow in the Easter Parade...
Oh, I could write a sonnet about your Easter bonnet,
And of the girl I'm taking to the Easter Parade.

**Written by Irving Berlin and sung by Judy Garland
in the film *Easter Parade***

You will need:
Large paper plates
Crayons, markers, paints
Sequins, bits of old lace, glitter-stick, feathers, etc
Glue
Elastic or ribbon

Children can decorate a paper plate any way they wish by sticking on paper flowers, drawing and painting on the plate, sprinkling glitter etc. Pierce a hole on either side of the plate and thread through pieces of ribbon or elastic to be tied under the chin to hold the bonnet on.

To Grow a Cress Family

Do this on a day when you are planning to make scrambled eggs or to make a cake. And, if you want them in time for Easter, make sure you 'plant' them seven or eight days ahead.

Carefully top and empty six eggs. Wash the eggshell (keep the insides for scrambled eggs). Then gently stuff them with cotton wool. Dampen the cotton wool by gradually tipping a teaspoonful of water onto it and then tipping the egg so that the water that hasn't soaked in drains out. Put the eggs into an egg box and then sprinkle half a teaspoon of cress or mustard seeds onto the damp cotton wool in each egg. Put the eggs onto a windowsill, or anywhere in the light, keep them damp and then watch the cress grow. Children can make a 'family' of cress eggs, drawing their faces on the shells with felt pen or crayon.

To Make a Pop-up Easter Card

You will need:
A piece of card, envelope size when folded in two
An old envelope
Crayons and felt pens
PVA glue

Fold the card in half. Crease the fold well, then open it out again. Cut the corner off an old envelope so you have a little pocket about half an inch square. This is going to be the Easter chick's beak. Get the children to crayon it inside and out. Then glue the beak into the centre of the open card, halfway down the centre crease. Next, lift the top of the beak, closing the card as you do so. Rub across the closed card to flatten the beak. Open the card again and the children can draw a chick head and body around the beak, not forgetting eyes, and pin men legs and feet. The rest of the card around the chick can be 'customised' by the children with crayoned flowers, grass or any other decoration they think fun. When the card is opened the beak will pop open too.

Egg and Spoon Race

Not a traditional Easter sport, but a good way to let off steam after all that chocolate. It can be played with real hard-boiled eggs or the chocolate kind.

Decorating Eggs

To decorate eggs you need to work on either hard-boiled or blown eggs. Blowing eggs needs patience and some skill and is only suitable for older grandchildren, or you. If you want to keep your decorated eggs as mementos, blown eggs it must be. However, blown eggs are more fragile and harder for children to handle.

Duck eggshells are tougher, slightly larger and their beautiful bluish tinge makes a good background for egg painting. Otherwise hen's eggs are perfectly good. Keep the box they come in for putting each egg to dry after painting. A box of half a dozen decorated eggs, the carton itself, painted in poster paint and with a message from a child drawn on the lid, makes a wonderful Easter present.

To Blow an Egg

Yes, granny, it's your turn to teach someone how to suck eggs.

Carefully poke a small hole in each end of the egg with a large darning needle or bodkin. Push the needle into the egg and twist it around to break the yoke. Hold the egg over a bowl and blow hard through the top hole until the shell is empty. Wash the empty eggshells carefully and allow them to dry. Save the raw eggs and scramble them for breakfast.

A dear friend who used to whip children into a frenzy of excitement at every possible occasion, had a theory that if you threw an egg (raw of course) right over the house, it wouldn't break. The breakage rate proved him wrong again and again, but everyone had a wonderful time.

Dyeing Eggs

You will need:
Food colouring from any supermarket – cochineal, yellow, green etc
White vinegar, to set the colour
A small saucepan
Slotted spoon

Place the eggs and several teaspoons of food dye into a saucepan of water with a tablespoon of white vinegar and bring slowly to the boil. For hard-boiled eggs, cook for nine minutes.

Sponge Painting Eggs

You will need:
Eggs, hardboiled or blown
Non-toxic poster paints
Saucers (for each colour)
Finger-sized pieces of sponge cut from a kitchen sponge
Large safety pins (one for each colour)
Eggcups
Old biros

Place the prepared eggs in eggcups. Partially fill saucers with various colours of paint. Clip a very small piece of bath sponge to a safety pin and dip into the paint, using the safety pin as a handle. Lightly dab the sponge over the top half of the egg. Let dry. Turn egg over and repeat procedure. Let the egg dry completely. You can then dab a second colour randomly on top to give a pretty, mottled effect.

Remove and discard the inner filament of an old biro and carefully press a tiny ball of kitchen sponge into the hole at the pointed, writing end of the biro casing. You then have a sponge paint brush, which can be dipped into the paint and dabbed gently onto the eggshell for more delicate decoration, and even for writing on people's initials.

HALLOWE'EN

When I was a child, the nearest we got to celebrating Hallowe'en was having to go to Church the day after, on All Saints' Day (1 November). There were no parties, no dressing up as witches and ghosts, and definitely no trick-or-treating. Call me Granny Spoilsport, but I am rather dismayed by the American custom, imported in the 20th century, of children going round knocking on strangers' doors and blackmailing them into handing out sweets.

Grandparents of a nervous disposition draw their curtains on Hallowe'en, switch off the lights and pretend there is nobody at home – in itself quite a spooky experience. Braver grandparents, or those who live in nicer neighbourhoods, keep a big bowl of sweets by the front door to hand out to the pint-sized ghoulies, ghosties and skeletons who come calling. But however they feel about Hallowe'en customs, good grannies are always willing to enter into the spirit of the preparations with gusto. Some ideas are outlined below.

Dressing Up and Props

To Make a Witch's Hat

You will need:
2 large sheets of black card, not too stiff
A sharp cutting knife, or Stanley knife
Scissors
Silver tinsel or wool for the witch's hair
A stapler, or tough electrical tape
A tape measure

1] Measure the child's head and allow an inch or so extra for the necessary join.

2] Cut the card into a large triangle shape, with a curving bottom edge, which should equal the child's head measurement (see above).

3] Bend this into a cone shape and staple, or tape with masking tape up the inside. Place this cone in the centre of the second piece of paper.

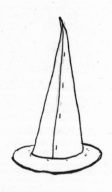

4] To make the brim of the hat, draw a circle around the outside of the cone on the paper with marker pen and then remove the cone.

5] Then draw a second, outer circle 3 or 4 inches from the first, either freehand or using a large round dish as template. You should be left with a kind of halo, marked on the card, which, once cut out, will form the brim of the hat. Use a sharp cutting knife to score around the lines and then press out the circular 'brim'.

6] Take the cone and insert it through this 'brim', so that the bottom inch or so of the cone is showing below the paper plate 'brim'.

7] Cut small slits every few inches in this sticking out part to make tabs and then fold them and tape them securely with masking tape to the underneath of the 'brim'. You now have the hat.

8] Decide the length of your witch's hair and add a few extra inches for taping it to the inside of the hat. Cut the tinsel into lengths. Tape the ends of tinsel up under the inside edge of the cone, leaving the front of the hat free for the witch's face. The hat can then be decorated with glitter and moons and stars cut out of kitchen foil. Quality Street or similar cellophane and coloured foil sweet wrappers, cut or scrunched up, look very glittery and effective when stuck onto the hat with a dab of glue.

9] Black material can be attached to the witch's shoulders as a cloak.

10] Use baby powder to make a ghoulish white face or use face paints.

The witch might be accompanied by a black cat. The 'cat' could wear black tights and a long sleeved black tee shirt. Its tail could be the leg of a pair of black tights stuffed with other old tights and safety-pinned on. Use a black hair band with two small triangles, cut out of cardboard for the 'ears' – paint them black and glue them to the hair band. Paint some whiskers on the face with eyeliner or face paint, to complete the ensemble. The witch might like to carry a witch's (garden) broom.

A Wizard and A Spider

The cone shape of the witch's hat, minus the brim, and with some extra silver foil crescent moons, makes a perfect wizard's hat.

A small grandson might like to be a Halloween spider. Dress him entirely in anything black and then attach 'spiders legs' to his back.

The legs can be made from a pair of black tights, stuffed with other old tights or scrumpled newspaper. Sew, or staple the ends to keep the stuffing from falling out. Attach the legs to his clothing by sewing or with safety pins. A balaclava, again cut out of old black tights, and some ski goggles complete the spider.

A Luminous Hallowe'en Skeleton

You need black opaque tights, a long-sleeved tee shirt and white iron-on backing fabric. Draw the outline of a very basic skeleton in separate pieces – legs, arms and ribs and cut them out in the backing fabric. The children can colour them in a luminous green. Iron these onto the front of the black tights and tee shirt and complete the costume with black gloves and socks.

Wands for Witches and Wizards

Place a long wooden spoon on some kitchen foil and wrap it up into a silver wooden spoon shape, securing with sellotape. Cut out two identical star shapes in stiff card. They should be larger than the 'spoon' end. Glue silver foil onto the 'stars'. Then attach a 'star' to either side of the 'spoon' end, using double-sided sellotape. Staple the points together to make them into one star. A witch might like streamers of black ribbon tied around her wand, underneath the 'star'.

Tip: Put outfits and accessories in Granny's Dressing Up Box for next time.

Pumpkin Lantern

Cut a circular hole around the stalk of the pumpkin, tilting the point of the knife into the centre of the pumpkin. This will stop the lid from falling in.

Scoop out the seeds and any loose flesh using a dessertspoon and knife. Sketch the face on to your pumpkin. Use a biro so any mistakes can be scrubbed off with a scouring pad or fingernail.

Carefully cut out the features. Take small cuts and use a puncturing motion rather than a slicing one. Gently scrape away the flesh on the inside of the face until it is only 1cm thick.

Using the knife, mark a circle the size of your candle or tea-light in the centre of the base. Carefully hollow out the marked area with the teaspoon and place your candle in the hollow; light it, and re-place the lantern lid.

A Hallowe'en Cocktail

You will need:
An orange for each child
1 or 2 tins fruit cocktail, depending on numbers
Seedless grapes
1 black magic marker

Cut the tops off the oranges, as if you were preparing a Hallowe'en pumpkin. Scoop out the inside, being careful not to damage the peel. Chop up the scooped-out orange to use with the fruit mixture. Using the magic marker draw Hallowe'en faces on the oranges. Let them dry. In a large bowl mix the fruit salad, seedless grapes and the orange pieces. Scoop this mixture into the oranges and chill for at least an hour.

Toffee Apples

6 small sweet apples
6 wooden skewers
8oz/225g granulated sugar
4fl oz/120ml water

1oz/30g butter

2 tbsp golden syrup

Push the wooden sticks halfway into the apples at the stalk end.

Mix the sugar and water in a thick-bottomed pan and dissolve the sugar over a gentle heat. Add the butter and syrup and bring to the boil. Boil without stirring until the toffee reaches the soft-crack stage, which is 290°C – measured on a sugar thermometer or when a piece of the mixture dropped into cold water forms into a ball.

Remove from the heat. Dip the apples into the toffee, one by one. Make sure each apple is well coated and leave to harden on a baking tray lined with baking parchment.

Hallowe'en Games

Pumpkin Quoits

You will need:

3 or 4 large, long-necked butternut squash pumpkins

Marker pens

Hoops or Deck Quoits (you could use a hollow Frisbee for this, or even make some out of garden wire and strong DIY tape)

Give each of the squashes a different point value and mark it on the squash clearly with magic marker. Then arrange them in a diagonal line, the highest score furthest from a starting line.

Players stand on the starting line and try to toss a hoop around a pumpkin – several tries for each child. The highest score wins.

Witch's Cauldron Game

You will need:
A cauldron (a large bowl)
Old cardboard eggbox cups (one fewer than the number of children)
Magic Marker pens in 2 different colours
Score sheet
Pen
Witch's hat

Carefully slice the cups from an egg box (to end up with a small walnut-sized cup, just under an inch high), and mark a dot of one colour in one half of the cups and the other colour in the second half.

The children should sit in a circle, around the cauldron with the eggcups lying flat side down inside it so they can't see their colours. One child wears the witch's hat. All the others pick a cup, keeping the colour a secret. The 'witch' tries to guess the colour of each child's cup in turn. A child must try hard to help the witch 'see' their colour by concentrating on it. After the witch makes a guess, the child reveals their colour. Finally, the number of correct guesses is added up, and the game starts again with the next 'witch'. When everyone has been 'witch', the player who was able to 'see' the most colours correctly is pronounced 'the winner'.

Apple Bobbing

Put a large bowl of water on the floor and float some apples in it. The children kneel down with their hands behind their backs and pick up apples with their teeth. The aim is to see who can pick up the most apples within a particular time limit. It can be very messy so be well prepared, with towels, etc, and use small apples to make it easier.

On Hallowe'en if you peel an apple, so that the peel is all in one piece, and throw it over your shoulder while looking in the mirror, it is supposed to land in the shape of the initial of your true love's name. Combine clairvoyance with getting your grandchildren to help make an apple pie.

CHRISTMAS

Christmas is without any doubt the highlight of every child's year, stretching out for weeks before the big day and several days after it. Sharing their anticipation and enjoyment gives grandparents great pleasure too. Pre-Christmas is a time when grandparents and grandchildren can enter a conspiracy to surprise and delight the rest of the family.

Decorations

Christmas Wreath

A big paper plate
Green and/or red and silver poster paint
Paintbrushes
Scissors
PVA glue
Glitter, tinsel, sequins, and pictures of Christmas things cut out
of magazines
Some trailing ivy and greenery (bay, laurel and mistletoe are
not prickly like holly, and are just as traditional)

Cut out the centre of the paper plate, leaving only the outside ring.
Paint it a colour – green, silver, red, then stick on the decorations.
Make a hole with a hole puncher at the top and thread through some
Christmas ribbon to hang the wreath by.

A Christmas Log

Choose an attractive log, at least a foot long and five or six inches
in diameter. Make sure that it will balance on a flat surface. Coat it
lightly with glue and frost it with glitter. Leave it to dry. Then, with
a knife, make small impressions on the top of the log to form bases
for candles or night lights... Bind the log round with red ribbon and
insert small evergreen branches under the ribbon which will keep
them in place.

Light a candle, and allow the wax to drip into the impressions you have made so the candles can sit comfortably on the log. Fix them on carefully. You can twine ivy around their bases. Glue on or fix with blu-tack some pieces of holly, fir cones and small bundles of cinnamon sticks.

Frosty Fir Cones

You will need fir cones, a can of silver, white or gold spray paint, and some pretty ribbon.

This couldn't be easier, and is very effective – just watch that the spray paint does not miss its target. Spray the fir cones, either uniformly, or in swirls and stripes, and then use the ribbon to make loops round the cones so that they can be attached to tree branches.

Christmas Puffballs

These are made out of tissue paper and can be hung on thread from the tree.

You will need
About ten sheets of tissue paper in different colours (good grannies save tissue paper wrapping all the year round) and/or cellophane
A small saucer – for example, the saucer of a coffee cup
A pencil

Scissors
Needle and thread

Place the saucer over the ten sheets of tissue paper and trace a circle round its base in pencil. Cut out the circle, cutting through all ten layers. Take one circle at a time fold it in half and then in half again. Now take a needle and thread and poke it through the point of each triangle until they are all suspended on the same length of thread. Tie the thread tightly. Leave enough thread to form a hanging loop and open out the triangles to form the puffball.

Tip: Experiment with different colour combinations. Alternating triangles of cellophane and tissue paper in the same ball looks very Christmassy. For extra glamour, spray the edges with gold or silver.

Button and Felt Tree Decorations

You will need:
Two or three sheets of bright coloured felt – a dayglo colour like pink or yellow, mixed with two more sombre colours, such as French grey, burgundy, blue-black or bottle green work well
Some old buttons
Good bits of ribbon
A little bit of polyester stuffing
Old newspaper to cut patterns
Embroidery thread and an embroidery needle

The idea is to make some lightly padded felt tree decorations, such as miniature Christmas stockings (which can hold a wrapped sweet, or something similar), or hearts, or stars, stitched in simple running stitch in a fun embroidery colour, and adorned with buttons and ribbon bows. It makes an ideal first sewing project for a keen eight or nine-year-old, and the end results are surprisingly pretty and effective.

For the Christmas stockings: take some newspaper and draw a simple stocking shape, about four–five inches high; pin the pattern to your chosen felt and cut it out twice (this might be something for Granny to take charge of, as messy cutting will show in the final stocking).

Sew the two felt stocking shapes together, using a fairly generous running stitch (or use oversewing stitch). Keep within a quarter of an inch from the edge. Be careful not to sew across the top of your stocking if you want to put a sweet or little present into it!

Now you are ready to decorate the stocking – again take care not to sew through both pieces of material. Make a little gingham bow, and sew this on to the toe; sew a selection of pearly buttons at random all over it; take some glittery ribbon and sew it round the top of the stocking, about half an inch from the top, to look like a garter or fold down edge.

Finally, sew a loop (about seven/eight inches should be enough) of ribbon to one side of the top circular rim of the stocking, with which to hang it on a branch of your tree; stuff a bit of the polyester padding into the toe, and then pop a brazil toffee Quality Street in, so that the purple shiny wrapping is just protruding from the top.

For the hearts and star shapes, cut a pattern from newspaper for each, aiming at about three inches wide/high for both. Sew the two sides of felt together, leaving a hole just large enough to be able to stuff some wadding in. Finish the sewing, and decorate. Sew a ribbon loop to the tip of one prong of the star, or to the top crease in the heart, to hang it on the tree.

Paper Chains

They may not add to the elegance of your Christmas décor, but children still love making paper chains to hang from one corner of a room to another.

You will need:
**Sheets or a roll of strong brown wrapping paper (or use up
    colourful old wrapping paper or left-over wallpaper)
Poster paints in red and green
Paintbrushes
Glitter sticks
Kitchen foil
Scissors, glue sticks and a hole punch**

Paint some of the wrapping paper green all over and some red, or buy ready-made sheets of paper in these colours. The third sheet should be stroked all over with glue sticks and stuck with silver foil dots made with the hole puncher or, simply ready-made dots that are sold on cards at stationery shops.

Cut all the sheets into strips about 8 by 1 ½ inches and make chains, sticking the edges together with glue stick, or stapling them.

Crackers

Christmas wouldn't be Christmas without them, my family say when I complain about what poor value they are. I've spent the aftermath of too many Christmasses picking bits of trashy plastic toy out of the Hoover's innards or the dog's jaws. If you, too, are sick of paying through the nose for boxes of ornate crackers with rubbishy knick-knacks inside that nobody wants, and jokes or riddles even more feeble than Uncle Bob's, amuse your grandchildren by getting them to make their own.

Start early, saving lavatory paper inner tubes.

You also need:
Sweets, to put inside the cracker
Tissue paper
Sheets of jolly Christmas wrapping paper – patterned or plain
 silver foil
Scissors, glue and sellotape
Optional 'snaps', obtainable from
 specialist shops

Give each child a cardboard tube and a sweet to put inside it. They can also write little jokes or riddles on pieces of paper to be put in with the sweet.

If you are using snaps, put them in at this stage, making sure they stick out at each end. Then stuff crumpled tissue paper into either end of the tube so that the sweet is secure in a little nest in the centre. Put the tube on the Christmas paper and cut out a rectangle of paper all round the tube, leaving an overlap to stick down and allowing two or three inches each end for the cracker 'frills'.

Roll the paper around the tube and stick it down the side with glue or tape. Fluff out the 'frills' and staple around the 'neck'. Finally glue a little collar of silver foil or contrasting paper over the indented neck. Or tie two narrow pieces of ribbon in bows around it.

Christmas Presents
to Make or Grow

Hyacinths or Narcissi for Mum

To grow and decorate a pot of Christmas bulbs could be a wonderful, secret project for you and your grandchildren and a lovely 'surprise' for their mother.

Buy prepared, pre-forced hyacinth bulbs and help the children to plant them by the end of September to have them flowering in time for Christmas. Show the children pictures so that they can choose the colours they like, and help them choose a pot or bowl. A plastic pot would be cheaper and could be wrapped in Christmas paper and tied with a bow at the end of the project. A small clay flowerpot with three hyacinths or six narcissi will be charming too and the children can decorate it with poster paints.

Put some compost at the bottom of the bowl or pot and place the bulbs on it. A 6in diameter pot will hold 3 hyacinths, 6 narcissi, or 12 crocuses. The bulbs should be close together, but should not touch each other nor touch the sides of the container: and don't force the bulbs down into the compost.

Fill the pot with more compost, pressing it firmly but not too tightly around the bulb. When finished, the bulb tips should be just above the surface and there should be about ½ in between the top of the compost and the container. Water the compost so that it is damp but not soggy.

Put the pots in a cold dark place. Children will enjoy peeping occasionally to make sure that the compost is still moist and to see the bulbs start into growth.

When the shoots are one to two inches tall move the pot into a cool (50°F) room in the house. Put the pots in a shaded spot at first and gradually move them into full light over a few days. In a couple of weeks flower buds will start to form. When the buds start to colour the pots can be moved to a warmer position, bright, but not sunny, away from draughts and not too near a radiator. Keep the compost damp at all times and turn the pot occasionally.

Hyacinths in Water

This is good fun for children, as they can watch the roots of the bulbs developing.

For a container try a glass carafe or anything with a narrow enough neck for the bulb to be held above the water. Some nurseries and mail order companies sell special hyacinth glasses.

Fill the glass with water, but not so full that the water is in contact with the bulb, adding a fragment of charcoal to keep the water sweet.

Set the bulb, nose uppermost, on the neck of the glass. Store in a cool dark place (45–48°F). A shelf in the garage or a cellar is ideal. Top up the water when needed. The children can check on their bulb every so often and make sure that the water stays just millimetres away from the bottom of the bulb. When the bulb's shoot has grown two inches high, bring the bulbs into light (not direct sunlight) and watch them grow and bloom.

Paperwhite narcissus can be grown in the same way, and will flower in six weeks. They will also grow in a bowl of pebbles or gravel. All they need is water.

Just before Christmas, wrap the plant, or tie a ribbon around it and make a label.

A Spectacles or Mobile Phone Case

You will need:
Felt (approx 1 ft/30cm square)
Embroidery cotton and needle

You can buy felt at a local craft shop. See whether they have off-cuts.

For the right size, get a real glasses case or phone and help the children to measure it. Then, make a paper pattern this size, roughly six inches by two and a half inches. Allow plenty of room in the measurements for childish sewing (or glueing). Fold the piece of felt in half, lengthways and pin the pattern to it so that the folded side makes one complete edge of the 'case'. Cut around the other sides and mark a line for the stitching. Sew using backstitch or oversewing stitch, or glue everything together – leaving one end open, of course.

It can be decorated by sticking on felt pieces or braid.

A Paperweight

Forward planning applies here: look out for suitable large, smooth stones when beachcombing earlier in the year. Children can paint, stencil or write a message on them – maybe the name of the recipient or the year. A small piece of felt can be cut out and glued to the underside.

A Small Album for Photographs or Notes

You will need;
**2 sheets of corrugated cardboard, about 7in by 9in, for the
cover and the back
12 sheets of A4 paper cut in half for the inside
A hole puncher
Some coloured string or ribbon to lace the 'album' together**

Punch three corresponding holes in both pieces of the cardboard cover and punch matching holes in the paper inside leaves. Then lace these holes together using the string, starting and finishing with the middle hole on the front. Finally knot the string and tie it in a bow.

The children can draw a title on the front cover and decorate it.

A Christmas Card Jigsaw Game

For children to make for granny, or for granny to make for them.

Collect old Christmas cards and cut them into big pieces in interesting shapes. Put them inside a small box or an envelope, which you have decorated. Wrap them up. When the present is opened, the pieces are tipped out – onto a tray or the floor, and the game is to match and reassemble them as quickly as possible.

EPIPHANY

If you have a Christmas crib, the Epiphany, on 6 January, is the day the Three Kings are placed beside the crib. This is traditionally when the Three Wise Men from the East arrived with presents of gold, frankincense and myrrh for the Infant. It is also Twelfth Night, the day that Christmas decorations should be taken down and stored until the following Christmas.

The French make a special Epiphany Cake, Galette des Rois, in which they hide a small china figure of a king or, sometimes, a bean. They place a cardboard crown on top of the cake and when it is sliced whoever gets the bean or china figure in their slice is king or queen for the day and wears the crown.

Epiphany Cake *(from the French Embassy)*
Serves 8

> 1¹/₄ **lb/550g frozen puff pastry**
> 2 **eggs**
> 7 oz **almond paste**

Preparation:
Leave the puff pastry at room temperature for about 2 hours until defrosted but still cold.

Preheat the oven to 200°C/gas mark 7.

Line a baking sheet or pizza pan with baking parchment or grease the pan and lightly sift flour on it. Shake off any excess flour. Roll each sheet of pastry into a circle about 12 inches across.

Place one circle on the prepared pan. Mix one egg with the almond paste until smooth and spread the mixture evenly on the prepared circle of pastry, leaving a border $1^1/_2$ inches wide all around. As you are unlikely to have a small china king, you can use a dried broad or butter bean, or perhaps a brazil nut; insert it into the almond mixture. Place the second circle of pastry on top and press it down tightly around the rim.

Beat lightly the remaining egg and brush it on the top of the cake. With a long-bladed knife, press lightly but firmly through the egg glaze marking a crisscross pattern.

Bake for 20–25 minutes until golden and puffed. Do not check for doneness for at least 15 minutes, as the pastry may collapse. Serve slightly warm or cold.

GUY FAWKES AND BONFIRE NIGHT

Remember, remember, the fifth of November
With gunpowder treason and plot
I see no reason why gunpowder treason
Should ever be forgot.

Tell your grandchildren the story behind Bonfire Night:

In 1605 thirteen conspirators, led by Robert Catesby, plotted to blow up King James I and the House of Parliament. One of the conspirators wrote to a friend, warning him to stay away from Parliament. His letter reached the king and, on 5 November, a search was made. Guy Fawkes was found in a cellar beneath the House of Lords, with 36 barrels of gunpowder. The arrest of Guy Fawkes and the prevention of the plot are commemorated every year with fireworks and bonfires on which his effigy is burned.

Most towns and large villages celebrate 5 November with a bonfire and a firework display, if not on the day, on the nearest weekend. It might be fun to take the grandchildren, but the very young may not like the bangs. If you don't want to go to a large, organised affair, go to the other extreme: just buy a packet of sparklers and light them in the garden at home. If you have room for a bonfire, bake potatoes in the hot ashes for supper.

SHROVE TUESDAY

Pancake Day is always on the day before Ash Wednesday, which marks the beginning of Lent. Lent is the period of fasting before Easter, and in the olden days even eggs were forbidden, so it became traditional to use up all of the household's eggs before Lent began, by making pancakes. The day is also known as Mardi Gras, French for 'Fat Tuesday', to mark the last consumption of eggs, butter and cream before Lent begins.

In some countries Mardi Gras is celebrated with three days of

Carnival with dancing and partying all day and all night. The most famous of all the Mardi Gras carnivals is in Rio de Janeiro in Brazil.

My grandchildren have pancakes for breakfast at weekends, so they are not such a special treat, but we still have them on Shrove Tuesday, filled with lemon and sugar, chocolate spread or maple syrup.

♥3♥
Food Glorious Food...

I don't know who loves food more — me or my grandchildren. When they arrive at our house, 'Granny can we make something?' is often their first question. 'Something' may be a pizza, a cake, biscuits, pancakes, gingerbread men or fudge. Whatever the ultimate product, cooking together is not only one of the best ways to enjoy their company, it also lays the foundations for their being helpful at home and able to look after themselves properly in later life.

But there are times when you won't feel in the mood for the hassle and mess that cooking with children inevitably involves. If you have been with them all day, or even just for an afternoon, you will be knackered by supper time. The following recipes — ten savoury dishes, ten puddings, and a range of snacks — besides being quick and easy, have two virtues. They include in palatable form various vegetables which might otherwise not go down without an argument. And granny and grandpa will enjoy eating them too.

TOP TEN EASY SUPPERS

Celery raw develops the jaw
But celery stewed
Is more quietly chewed.
Ogden Nash

Spaghetti with Peas, Lardons and Crème Fraiche
Serves 4

12oz/350g spaghetti
1 tbsp of olive oil
1 onion, chopped
A packet of lardons
Half a small packet of frozen petit pois
A small carton of crème fraiche
A handful of grated parmesan

Bring a large pan of water to the boil, add a good pinch of salt and the spaghetti and cook according to the directions on the packet.

Meanwhile heat the oil in a frying pan, cook the onions until soft, then add the lardons. Cook for five minutes.

Now add the peas and crème fraiche to the lardons and cook for a few more minutes until the peas are tender. Stir the mixture into the spaghetti. Season with salt and pepper, adding a little more crème fraiche if it is too dry. Sprinkle with grated parmesan.

Tuna Fish Bake with Sweet Corn

Serves 2

    1 large or 2 small tins of tuna
    A large tin of sweet corn
    3 tomatoes sliced
    1oz/30g flour
    1oz/30g butter
    $^3/_4$ pint/450ml milk
    A tablespoon grated cheddar cheese

Set the oven at 180°C/gas mark 4. Put the tuna and sweet corn into an ovenproof pie dish and cover with the tomato slices. Make a white sauce and pour it over the mixture. Then sprinkle the grated cheese on top and bake in the oven for 30 minutes.

Variation: use tinned wild salmon instead of tuna.

Spicy Chicken Drumsticks

Preparation of this dish is incredibly simple, but it does have to be planned in advance, to allow the marinade to work its magic.

    1 or more free-range chicken drumsticks or
        thighsper child, depending on their age
    2 cloves of garlic
    Juice of 1 lemon
    3 tbsp Soy sauce

Set the oven at 190°C/gas mark 5. You can use thighs or drumsticks for this, or a mixture of both. Put them in a shallow, oven-proof dish. With a sharp, pointed knife, make slits in the chicken skin and tuck slivers of garlic into the slits. Mix the lemon juice with the Soy sauce and pour it over the chicken pieces. Cover the dish in foil and leave in the fridge to marinate overnight. Bake for 45 minutes.

Pitta Pockets
Serves 4

White bread, only available at Granny's house, is considered a great treat by my grandchildren. For some reason they also love nutritious wholemeal pitta bread and don't regard it as 'brown'.

4 pitta breads
1 or 2 sausages per child
Tomatoes, sliced
Celery
Lettuce leaves
Sliced cucumber
Tomato ketchup

Grill the sausages. Toast the pitta bread in a toaster, cut each slice in half and open up to make 'pockets'. Spread tomato ketchup on the inside of the pocket, then line it with some tomato slices, celery, and lettuce leaves and put a sausage in the middle.

Courgette Boats

Serves 2

2 large courgettes
1 onion, finely chopped
$^1/_2$ lb/230g minced beef
2 eggs, beaten
3 tbsp parmesan
A handful finely chopped parsley
Salt and pepper
1 tbsp breadcrumbs
2oz/60g butter

Set the oven at 200°C/gas mark 6. Parboil the courgettes in a pan of boiling water until soft (about 5 minutes), then drain. Cut them lengthways in half and scoop out the insides. Brown the onion and minced beef in butter, add a little water and cook for about 20 minutes.

Allow to cool, then add the 2 beaten eggs, 2 tbsps of parmesan, parsley, salt and pepper. Put this mixture into the courgette halves and sprinkle with the breadcrumbs mixed with the remaining parmesan. Bake the courgettes on an oiled baking tray for 30 minutes.

Cauliflower Cheese with Breadcrumb Topping

Serves 4

Strangely, although broccoli is popular with most children (they enjoy its resemblance to miniature trees), naked cauliflower is not, and they're canny enough not to be fooled by the description 'white broccoli'. My sympathy is all with them. As a child I was made to eat up insipid, flabby, watery cauliflower, and loathed it. I had no idea it was related to delicious cauli cheese with its crunchy topping.

For the cauliflower cheese:
1 cauliflower
$1^3/_4$ oz / 50g butter
2 tablespoons flour
$3/_4$ pint / 450ml milk
$3^1/_2$ oz / 100g grated cheese
$1/_2$ teaspoon mustard
A pinch of nutmeg

For the breadcrumb topping:
4 slices brown bread
3oz / 75g butter
Salt and freshly ground black pepper

Set the oven at 220°C/gas mark 7. Cut the cauliflower into florets, and steam for five minutes until just tender. Meanwhile, melt the butter in a saucepan, and add the flour, stirring constantly for 1 or 2 minutes. Gradually add the milk (you may not need it all), the grated cheese, mustard and nutmeg and stir until smooth. Put the cauliflower into an oven dish, and pour the sauce over.

For the topping, melt butter in frying pan and add breadcrumbs. Cook over a moderately high heat, stirring until crunchy. Season with salt and pepper and sprinkle over the cauliflower cheese.

Vegetable Fish Pie

Serves 4

1$^1/_2$ lbs/700g mixed vegetables, e.g. carrots, broccoli, peas
1lb/450g white fish
1$^1/_2$ lbs/700g potatoes
2 medium onions, finely chopped
2 rashers bacon, cut into small pieces
2oz/60g butter
A handful of grated cheese
Salt and pepper

Set the oven at 220°C/gas mark 7. Cook the vegetables in salted water; and poach or steam the fish and set aside. Cook the potatoes in salted water. Meanwhile, melt 1oz butter in a frying pan and fry the bacon and onions until soft. Chop the mixed vegetables finely and add them to the onion and bacon mixture.

Remove any bones or skin from the fish. Layer the vegetables and fish in a medium-size, buttered pie dish. Mash the potatoes with the remaining butter and a little milk. Spread the mashed potato over the fish and vegetables and sprinkle with grated cheese. Bake at the top of the oven, until browned on top.

Sticky Chops

Serves 6

Most children enjoy spicy food, and will love this sweet-and-sour devil sauce. Let them pick up the chops and gnaw the bones.

12 best end lamb chops, trimmed
2 tbsp Worcester sauce
2 tbsp tomato ketchup
2 tbsps vinegar
2 tbsps Soy sauce
The juice of 1 small lemon
2 tbsps brown sugar

Set the oven at 190°C/gas mark 5. Put the chops in a roasting tin. Mix together the Worcester sauce, tomato ketchup, vinegar and Soy sauce and pour over the chops. Squeeze the lemon juice over and sprinkle the brown sugar on top (you can use honey instead and adjust the amounts of sugar or honey according to your taste).

Bake in the oven for an hour or so, turning and basting the chops every 15 or 20 minutes, so they become well covered with sauce. If the sauce becomes too greasy, drain the fat off.

Variation: this works well with chicken pieces too.

Eggs in Baked Potatoes

Serves 4

[from Molly Keane's Nursery Cooking, Macdonald, 1985]

4 large potatoes
1oz/30g butter
2 tablespoons single cream or milk
Salt and pepper
4 eggs
2oz/60g grated cheese (optional)

Preheat the oven to 200°C/gas mark 6. Mark a circle round the top of each potato with the point of a sharp knife. Bake for about an hour until soft. Cut off the marked 'lid' and scoop out the potato flesh with a teaspoon, being careful not to pierce the skin. Mash the potato with the butter, cream and seasoning. Lower the oven temperature to 180°C/gas mark 4. Half fill the potato cases with the mixture, making a small well in the centre of each. Break an egg into each well, then return to the oven for 10–15 minutes or until the eggs are set. Pipe or spoon the remaining potato round the top, sprinkle with the cheese, if used, and brown under a hot grill.

Pasta with Boursin and Broccoli

Serves 2

In our family we frequently trade recipes. This one comes from our daughter Sophy and goes down a storm with her two boys, one of whom is, I have to admit, a bit of a fusspot. His favourite pasta is tagliatelle (I think it's because he loves saying the word) – but use whatever shape of pasta your grandchildren prefer.

Half a head of broccoli
6 'nests' of tagliatelle or equivalent amount of other pasta
1 small packet of Boursin garlic and herb cheese
2 tbsp of milk

Cut the broccoli into florets and boil it with the pasta. Melt the Boursin with a little milk or cream. Mix it all together and serve.

TOP TEN EASY PUDDINGS

To Granny's house I go
That I may fatter grow
The Story of Lambkin and his Drumkin
Anon

Yoghurt and Brown Sugar

Serves 4

It's all in the presentation – serving everyday ingredients in wine glasses makes them special.

1 large carton of plain yoghurt
1 tbsp of muscovado or barbados sugar

Divide the yoghurt between four glasses. Cover the top of the yoghurt with brown sugar and refrigerate until very cold.

Raspberry Ice Cream

Serves 4

Ice cream is a wonderful way to get fruit inside children who are put off by pips or skin.

I used to go through an elaborate Constance Spry method, whisking eggs and sugar for ages to achieve a mousse-like consistency. Quite unnecessary. This method, adapted from one in Tessa Hayward's book *Simply Ices*, is incredibly quick and quite delicious.

1lb/450g raspberries
4 oz/115g caster sugar
Juice of 1 lemon
$^{1}/_{2}$ pint/300ml whipping cream

Whiz the raspberries in a blender or food processor and sieve the purée to remove any pips. Add half the sugar and half the lemon juice and stir until the sugar is dissolved. Continue to add sugar and lemon juice until it tastes sweet enough, remembering that the cream will dilute the flavour. Stir the cream into the purée and freeze.

Variations: Any fruit can be treated in this way: strawberries, plums, damsons, blackcurrants, gooseberries, pineapple. The correct amount of sugar and cream is a matter of trial and error, depending on the sweetness of the fruit.

Tip: Invest in an ice cream scoop and serve the ice cream in wafer cornets – it's fun for the children and saves washing up.

Rice Pudding

Serves 4

'Lovely rice pudding for dinner again' was not my idea of fun, but when I was a child the recipe didn't include cream. It makes all the difference; so does jam or syrup as an accompaniment instead of boring old stewed fruit.

4oz/115g short-grain rice
$^3/_4$ pint/450ml milk
$^3/_4$ pint/450ml single cream
2oz/60g caster sugar
1 vanilla pod or 1 teaspoon vanilla extract
1 oz/30g hard butter, diced
Jam or syrup

Set the oven at 150°C/gas mark 2. Butter a pie dish. Put the rice, milk, cream, vanilla pod and sugar into the dish and give it a stir. Leave it for half an hour. Remove the vanilla pod, stir the mixture again and dot the butter over the top. Bake in the oven for about 3 hours, checking regularly to make sure the top does not burn. Children prefer this hot, I have found, with a dollop of strawberry jam, or a swirl of maple syrup.

Variation: If you are short of time (and rice pud does take 3 hours to cook) open a tin of Ambrosia Creamy Rice Pudding. Yes! They are still making the food of the gods, and have been since 1917. I hope I'm still around for the 100th anniversary. What's more, it's politically correct, and very nutritious, with no artificial colouring, flavouring or preservatives.

Baked Bananas in Honey

Serves 4

4 ripe bananas
4 teaspoons of soft brown sugar
1 lemon
4 teaspoons honey

Cut four squares of foil, big enough to wrap each banana. Place a peeled banana in the centre of each piece of foil. Sprinkle with sugar and add a little grated lemon rind. Squeeze lemon juice and a teaspoon of honey over each banana.

Make four sealed packets with the foil, place in the oven and cook for 10 minutes. Open the packets and serve. Very good with a little crème fraiche or vanilla ice cream.

Eton Mess

Eton Mess is a fool with attitude: a summery pudding which is about as easy as 'cooking' gets. When you use egg yolks to make custard, mayonnaise or hollandaise sauce, take ten minutes to whiz up the whites for meringues. They keep for months in an airtight container. Or use bought meringues.

Strawberries
Double cream
A few meringues

Hull the strawberries, put them in a bowl and roughly mash them with a fork. Whip the cream and roughly crumble the meringues. Fold everything together and serve in glasses for extra glamour.

Variation: According to season, use raspberries instead of strawberries, or cooked fruit such as rhubarb, gooseberries, blackcurrants or plums.

DIY Ice cream Sundae

As a special treat, let the children design and make their own ice cream sundaes. The worst part, for you, will be clearing up afterwards. There's no other work involved – it's a straightforward assembly job.

Vanilla ice cream
Strawberry ice cream
Chocolate ice cream
Squeezy bottles of sauce (chocolate, caramel, strawberry), or, for a slightly healthier option, Maple Syrup
Sprinkles
Choc chips
Wafers
Chopped fruit, or berries

Put all the ingredients on the table, give each child a shallow bowl, retire and watch from a safe distance.

Hot Chocolate Sponge

Serves 4

A cake, specially a chocolate cake, smells so wonderful when it comes out of the oven, that it seems a shame to wait for it to get cold before eating it. Time your baking so that you can eat it right away, as a pudding, with vanilla ice cream for the ultimate hot/cold experience.

6oz/175g self-raising flour
3 tbsp cocoa powder
1 tsp bicarbonate of soda
5oz/150g soft brown sugar
2 tbsp golden syrup
2 medium eggs, beaten
$^1/_4$ pint/150ml sunflower oil
$^1/_4$ pint/150ml milk
Apricot or raspberry jam
Vanilla ice cream

Set the oven to 180°C/gas mark 4. Grease and line two 18cm (7 inch) sandwich tins. Sieve the flour, cocoa and bicarbonate of soda into a bowl. Add the sugar and stir until mixed. Make a well in the centre and add the rest of the ingredients. Beat with a hand-held electric whisk until smooth.

Divide the mixture between the two tins and bake for 25 to 30 minutes. Spread jam on one half and put the other half on top. While the cake is still hot, serve it with the ice cream.

Peaches or Plums in Marmalade

Serves 4

> 4 large peaches, halved
> 4 tbsps orange marmalade
> 1¹/₂ oz/40g butter
> ¹/₄ tsp ground cinnamon
> 2 tbsps blanched almonds
> Whipped cream

Set the oven to 180°C/gas mark 4. Pour boiling water over the peaches to loosen the skins, and peel them. Halve them and arrange, cut side up, in a shallow baking dish.

Melt the marmalade, butter and cinnamon together in a saucepan, and pour the mixture over the peaches. Scatter the almonds on top. Cover and cook for 35 minutes. Serve hot with the cream.

Butterscotch Custard

Serves 4

> 2oz/60g dark, moist brown sugar
> 1oz/30g butter
> 1 tbsp golden syrup
> 1 pint milk
> 1¹/₂ oz/40g cornflour

In a saucepan, heat the butter, sugar and syrup and stir until dark brown but not burnt. In a small bowl or cup, make a paste with cornflour and a little of the milk. Add the rest of the milk to the butterscotch mixture in the saucepan. Heat the mixture to boiling point and add the cornflour, stirring all the time. Boil for 3 minutes.

Pour into a mould, which has been rinsed in cold water. Leave somewhere cool to set.

Mini Apple Tarts

Serves 4

A packet of puff pastry
3 or 4 eating apples, peeled and thinly sliced
2 teaspoons of honey

Set the oven at 200°C/gas mark 6. In a saucepan, cook the sliced apples gently with the honey until they are just soft. Taste and if they are not sweet enough, add a little more honey. Leave to cool.

Either use ready-rolled pastry, or roll out the pastry on a floured surface. Cut out rounds 5cm/2in diameter to line the tartlet tins. Put a few slices of apple in each tart.

Cut narrow strips from the pastry trimmings and lay them crisscross over the apple. Bake the tarts in the oven for 6–8 minutes until the pastry is golden.

THINGS TO MAKE WITH GRANNY

Grannies come into their own at teatime, remembering, as they do, the teatimes of their childhood with nostalgic affection. In case the art of making a proper cucumber sandwich or a Melting Moment is lost for ever, teach your grandchildren the technique.

Get out the tablecloth and the teapot, lay the table and do it all the way it used to be. Better still, spread a rug on the lawn and have a picnic tea in the garden, or put everything in a basket (including the sandwich crusts to feed the ducks) and go to the park.

Sandwiches

To cut properly thin slices of bread for the perfect sandwich, you need yesterday's loaf. The easiest way to butter the slices is to spread butter on the face of the loaf before cutting each slice. Small children enjoy cutting sandwiches into different shapes with cookie cutters. Among the sandwich fillings popular with my grandchildren are tuna with mashed avocado and Nutella or chocolate spread. Those described here are good old-fashioned granny favourites.

Marmite sandwiches

Cut thin slices of day-old white or brown bread, two for each sandwich. Butter lightly and then spread the marmite on top of one slice. Add a small bunch of watercress. Put the second buttered slice on top and cut the sandwich into four.

Perfect cucumber sandwiches

The thought of cucumber sandwiches conjures up pictures of Edwardian ladies presiding over silver teapots, sugar tongs, tea-leaf strainers and slop basins. Peel a cucumber, or part of it. Cut very thin slices using a potato peeler or a sharp knife. Put the slices to soak in a saucer of vinegar until you are ready to make the sandwiches. Butter and cut thin slices of white bread, and put a layer of cucumber onto one slice. Sprinkle on a little salt and some white pepper and put the second piece of buttered bread on top. Cut off the crusts and cut each sandwich into four triangles.

New Zealanders are said to eat marmite and crisp sandwiches, and some people like peanut butter and marmite sandwiches. In Australia they eat vegemite instead. Vegemite, which is similar to marmite, is so popular in Australia that the Australian Olympic team is up in arms because China isn't allowing vegemite in to Beijing.

My grandson, who likes marmite soldiers with his boiled eggs, learned this rhyme from his Australian class teacher:

> Twinkle, Twinkle Vegemite,
> Spread it on your toast at night.
> If you drop it on the ground,
> It will turn your carpet brown.
> Twinkle, Twinkle vegemite,
> I'm okay and you're alright.

Tomato sandwiches

Best made with brown bread. Pour boiling water over 3 or 4 tomatoes. Leave for a minute or so then remove the tomato skins. Slice tomatoes finely and season well with salt and white pepper. Butter and slice the bread and cover half the slices with tomato. Cover with the other slices of buttered bread and cut each sandwich into four. You can also mix a little mashed tinned sardine in with the tomato or some grated cheddar cheese.

Granny's chocolate sandwiches

Butter two slices of bread per person and arrange squares of chocolate evenly over half of them. Put them in the AGA, or in a very low oven, for 30 seconds before squishing another slice of buttered bread on top. To be eaten as a surprise treat for elevenses or tea.

Banana and honey spread

Mix 1oz of very soft butter and 1 tablespoon of honey in a bowl. Mash a banana with a fork and add to the mixture, stirring in well. Spread on a slice of bread and cut in four. This is specially enjoyed by the smallest children.

Toadstools

1 egg per child
$^1/_2$ tomato per child
$^1/_2$ cucumber
Mayonnaise

Hard boil an egg for each person, peel and leave to cool. Cut off the rounded ends of egg (top and bottom). Cut a tomato in half. Place the half tomato on top of the upright egg. Decorate with mayonnaise and surround with a few washed crisp lettuce leaves and some slices of cucumber.

A Smoothie

A glass of apple juice
1 banana
A large punnet of blueberries
A large punnet of blackberries
Juice of half an orange

Put into the blender and blitz.

CECILY: May I offer you some tea, Miss Fairfax? Sugar?
GWENDOLINE: [superciliously] No, thank you. Sugar is not fashionable any more.
[CECILY looks angrily at her, takes up the tongs and puts four lumps of sugar into the cup]
CECILY: [severely] Cake or bread and butter?
GWENDOLINE: [In a bored manner] Bread and butter please. Cake is rarely seen at the best houses nowadays.
CECILY: [cuts a large slice of cake and puts it on the tray] Hand that to Miss Fairfax.
[MERRIMAN does so, and goes out with footman. GWENDOLINE drinks the tea and makes a grimace; puts down cup at once, reaches out her hand to the bread and butter, looks at it and finds it is cake. Rises in indignation.]
GWENDOLINE: You have filled my tea with lumps of sugar, and though I asked most distinctly for bread and butter, you have given me cake. I am known for the gentleness of my disposition, and the extraordinary sweetness of my nature, but I warn you, Miss Cardew, you may go too far.

The Importance of Being Earnest **by Oscar Wilde**

Melting Moments

    4oz/115g butter, softened
    3oz/75g caster sugar
    1 egg yolk
    $^1/_2$ teaspoon vanilla extract
    4oz/115g self-raising flour
    About 2oz/60g porridge oats, crushed with a rolling pin

Line two baking trays with baking parchment. Put the oats on a plate or shallow dish. Beat the butter and sugar together until light and fluffy; beat in the egg yolk and vanilla, and stir in the flour. Work the mixture together lightly with your hands.

Then, using a teaspoon, form the dough into small balls and flatten them slightly with your palm. Put each little cake in the oats and coat it all over. Set the cakes well apart on the trays as they will spread to more than double their original size. Refrigerate for 20 minutes. Meanwhile, set the oven at 180°C/gas mark 4.

Bake the Moments for 15 minutes, and then leave to cool on a wire rack.

Frosted Redcurrants
[from Poor Cook, by Susan Campbell and Caroline Conran, Macmillan, 1971]

    1lb of ripe redcurrants still on their stems
    2 egg whites, whipped
    Caster sugar for coating

Place the egg whites in a bowl and lightly whip. Sprinkle plenty of caster sugar on a square of kitchen foil or greaseproof paper. Wash and dry the bunches of redcurrants and then dip them in the egg whites and then in the caster sugar. Lay them out to harden and dry, turning them over from time to time. Eat when they are ice cold on a hot summer's day.

Strawberry Water Ice

8oz/225g strawberries
Juice of 1 lemon
8oz/225g caster sugar
$^1/_4$ pint/6fl oz water
Grated orange rind
2 egg whites

Squeeze lemon juice over strawberries and sprinkle on a little caster sugar. Put in fridge for two hours.

Boil the caster sugar and water and grated orange rind for 10 minutes. Combine strawberries and syrup and liquidise. Put in freezer till fairly solid.

Now beat the egg whites until they are very stiff. Take the strawberry mixture out of freezer and gradually add a little bit at a time, breaking up the ice, to the egg whites.

Keep whisking until it is all mixed in. Freeze, and serve in glass tumblers on a lovely hot day.

Chocolate Crunchies

8oz digestive biscuits
4oz/115g icing sugar
10oz/285g good dark chocolate
8oz/225g butter
Smarties

Crumble biscuits then sift in the sugar and stir. Break the chocolate into pieces and put in the saucepan with the butter. Stir over a low heat until blended. Add the biscuit crumble and stir it in. Press this mixture into a greased tin and mark it into squares. Decorate it with smarties and leave it to set in the fridge for at least an hour.

Victoria Sponge Cake

This is the classic, can't-go-wrong cake recipe, made so much easier than it was in our days, by the invention of the food processor. But it's still essential to use softened butter, so remember to take it out of the fridge a couple of hours before you start.

You can vary it infinitely, substituting cocoa for part of the flour, adding grated lemon or orange rind and juice instead of vanilla for flavouring, or stirring in chocolate chips. The mixture can be used to make the classic cake in two layers, sandwiched with jam or butter icing, or for cup cakes or butterfly cakes. For children the best part is getting creative with icing and decorating, so stock up on food colouring, silver balls, smarties and hundreds and thousands.

3 eggs
unsalted butter, softened, the weight of the eggs
caster sugar, the weight of the eggs
self-raising flour, the weight of the eggs
1 teasp baking powder
$^1/_2$ tsp vanilla extract
2–3 tablespoons milk

Preheat the oven to 200°C/gas mark 6. Grease and line two 7in tins or set out 10 cup cake cases.

Put all the ingredients except the milk in a food processor and whiz, stopping as soon as the mixture is smooth. If it seems too stiff, pulse while adding the milk until it is a dropping consistency. Fill the cup cake cases or sandwich tins with the mixture.

Bake for 15–20 minutes (cup cakes), 25–30 minutes (sandwich cake) or until golden and springy to touch.

Really Useful Fool-proof Pastry

This pastry remains reasonably short and light even after being mauled in hot little paws and rolled out several times. It can be used for making pies and flans, as well as for little individual jam, lemon curd, treacle or custard tarts; or it can simply be cut out with pastry cutters to make the simplest kind of biscuits to ice and decorate.

3oz/85g ground almonds
3oz/85g plain flour
3oz/85g butter

Whiz the ingredients together in a food processor, adding a little water if needed. Wrap the dough in cling-film and chill for half an hour. Roll out on a floured surface and use as required. Bake at 190°C/gas mark 5.

Fruity Milk Shake

You can use almost any soft fruit for this – mango, peach, strawberry or raspberry pulp. It is a great way of using up fruit which is on the turn, and giving children a nutritious treat.

> 1 cup milk
> 2 scoops vanilla ice cream
> 4 large fresh strawberries (or $^1/_2$ cup frozen strawberries)
> 1 large banana, chopped
> 2–3 ice cubes

Blend together for one to two minutes.

Pizzas

For his last birthday my grandson invited a dozen friends to a cooking party. Among other delicious things, they made pizzas and ate them for tea. You can buy pizza dough and tomato sauce if you haven't got time to make your own.

1lb/500g strong white flour
2 tsps salt
1 sachet or 2 tsp yeast
about $^1/_2$ pint/300ml lukewarm water
2 tbsp olive oil
2 tsp sugar or honey

In advance: put the flour, salt and yeast in a bowl and stir to mix. In a jug, mix the oil and sugar or honey with the warm water. Make a well in the centre of the flour and gradually mix in the water mixture – you may not need it all. Mix it first with a wooden spoon, then with your hands.

Flour the work surface and knead the dough until it's smooth and stretchy. You need stamina for this. Put the dough back in the bowl, cover with cling film and leave for $1^1/_2$ to 2 hours until nearly doubled in size.

To make the pizzas, you will need:

The risen dough
4 paper plates

A choice of toppings, e.g.:

Tomato sauce (the easiest way to make this is to put
a tin of chopped tomatoes in a saucepan with a good
splash of olive oil, and simmer at medium heat until
reduced)
Grated cheese
Sliced pepperoni sausage
Sliced mushrooms
Sliced ham
Chopped herbs
Anchovies
Capers

Turn the oven to its hottest setting and put in a baking sheet. Flour
the worktop. Divide the dough into four and give a piece to each
child.

Let them knead and squidge it, then shape it into an approximate
disc with a rolling pin or their hands, with your help if needed. Put
each disc on a floured paper plate. Each child can now spread his
pizza with tomato sauce and add his favourite toppings.

Slide the pizzas off the plate on to the hot baking sheet (best done
by granny with everyone standing well clear). Cook the pizzas for 8
to 10 minutes, until the tops are sizzling and golden.

BRILLIANT BIRTHDAY CAKES

Birthdays and the celebratory cake are tremendously important to children. From my childhood I remember cakes made for my birthdays and those of my cousins. The most memorable were a Swan Lake scene with a mirrored lake and chocolate and white swans, and a princess with frosted redcurrants cascading down her crinoline skirt (see page 148).

Nowadays children's parties tend to have a theme, be it cowboys and Indians, knights and princesses or *Star Wars*. The children come appropriately dressed, and the birthday cake reflects the theme – a chance for Granny to amaze her family and their guests.

The Victoria sponge recipe given above can be expanded to make basic cakes of different sizes, which can then be cut and shaped into fantasy buildings or creatures. The principle is, always to use flour, butter and sugar of the same weight as the eggs. And just to give you an idea of volume: a 2 or 3-egg mixture will make a standard small round sponge; while a 7 or 8-egg mixture will fill a 9in cake tin.

However, some of the recipes below call for 9in square or round Madeira cakes, because Madeira is more solid than a fluffy sponge and easier to cut and carve; it will also keep longer, so can be made ahead, kept in the fridge and then iced and decorated near the day.

A simple Madeira recipe follows, with the correct amounts; then various useful icings, and finally the different, themed cakes.

Sponges, Icings and Fillings

Madeira Sponge (for a 9in square tin)

   13oz/365g softened butter
   13 oz/365g caster sugar
   8 eggs
   10 oz/285g plain flour
   3oz/85g self-raising flour
   2 tbsps milk

Preheat the oven to 160°C/gas mark 3. Prepare a 9in square tin, greasing it and lining it with baking parchment or greaseproof paper. Using a blender, beat the butter and sugar until light and fluffy. Add the eggs, one at a time, then fold in the sifted flour, and the milk. Spoon the mixture into the tin, smooth its surface and bake for about 1hr 40 mins.

Test the cake towards the end of the cooking time. Insert a skewer or knifepoint into the centre; if it comes out clean the cake is ready. Remove from the oven and leave to cool in the tin for at least 5 minutes before turning the cake out onto a wire rack.

You can store this cake in an airtight container in the fridge for up to two weeks, or freeze it for 2 months.

Victoria Sponge (for a 7in round tin)

(As on page 134 above)

Apricot Glaze

Use this before icing a cake with glacé or royal icing, to stop crumbs getting into the icing.

> **3 tbsp apricot jam, sieved**
> **1 tbsp lemon juice**

Heat the jam and lemon juice in a saucepan and push through a sieve into a bowl, using a wooden spoon. Spread this mixture on the cake, while still warm, but not too hot.

White Frosting

> **1oz/30g vanilla sugar**
> **$^1/_8$ pint/70 ml water**
> **7oz/200g granulated sugar**
> **1 egg white**

Put the sugars with the water into a saucepan and stir over a low heat until it has completely dissolved. Bring this to the boil. Continue to boil until a drop of the syrup makes a soft ball when dropped into cold water, or until it reaches 120°C measured with a thermometer. Then remove the pan from the heat. Whisk the egg white in a bowl until stiff and then pour in the syrup in a thin stream, whisking continuously until the mixture becomes very thick. Spread this over the cold cake with a spatula. It should be very white and light.

Glacé Icing

8oz/225g sieved icing sugar
2-3 tbsps hot water
Flavouring and colouring of choice

Mix the sieved icing sugar with the hot water gradually. Beat well until you obtain a smooth, coating consistency. Be cautious when adding the hot water as too much can make the icing too runny and your final ready-to-go mixture should seem a little stiff. Add any flavouring or colouring you wish.

Butter Icing

4oz/115g butter
10oz/285g icing sugar, sieved
1 tbsp orange or lemon juice or milk or water

Beat the butter and sugar together to a cream and beat in the flavour you want. The consistency should be smooth and creamy.

For vanilla add $^1/_2$ tsp vanilla essence; for chocolate, 2 level tbsp sieved cocoa powder, mixed to a paste with a little water; for lemon, 1 tsp lemon juice with a little grated peel.

NB – for pure white butter icing:
10oz/285g softened unsalted butter
10oz/285g sieved icing sugar
2 tbsp cold milk

Beat the butter until very soft and continue as for butter icing above, adding the milk and icing sugar alternately until they are used up, beating all the while. Continue until it is soft and white. This will give enough to cover a 9in cake.

Colourings

To colour the icing simply mix in a few drops of your chosen colour with the basic icing mixture. You can buy food colouring at any supermarket.

Chocolate Cream Filling

[from The Cook Book, Terence and Caroline Conran, Mitchell Beazley 1980]

3oz/85g dark chocolate
1oz/30g butter
1/4 pt double cream
5oz/150g icing sugar
Salt

Put the chocolate and butter into a bowl over a pan of hot water until they melt. Leave to cool. Mix in the cream, the icing sugar and a very small pinch of salt. Whisk with an electric mixer or by hand until thick.

Football Pitch Cake

Two 9 x 9in (23cm) Madeira cakes
Apricot glaze
Green glacé icing or green butter icing
Paper drinking straws
Tube of ready-made white icing
Subuteo football figures
One small white chocolate ball or truffle

Make the Madeira sponge as for the 9in square recipe above; when they are cool, cut a one inch strip off two adjoining sides of each of the sponges, to provide two 8in square pieces. Lay these sponge squares side by side on a large base – a cake board or chopping board, covered with foil – to make a football pitch-shaped cake 8 x 16in (20 x 40cm).

Cover the cake with an apricot glaze and then ice with glacé icing, coloured green, or with green butter icing, smoothed with a palette knife.

Cut goalposts out of straws, using icing to stick them together and place one goal at each end. Mark the pitch lines with a fine nozzle and a small amount of white glacé icing; alternatively you can make the pitch markings out of strips of liquorice 'bootlaces' or tiny silver balls.

Complete the scene with subuteo team figures and a small white chocolate 'ball' in the centre (white Maltesers are good for this; otherwise, a smooth white chocolate truffle).

Fort Cake

Two 9 x 9in (23cm) square Madeira cakes (as above)
Chocolate butter icing (made as above, with 15oz butter,
   enough to cover the equivalent of two 9-in cakes)
2 packets of Chocolate Finger biscuits
Boudoir biscuits (sponge fingers)
A single rectangular chocolate biscuit
A little beaten egg white
Brown sugar

Make two 9-in (23cm) square Madeira cakes. Cut one in half and put it aside. Then, on a large base – a tray, covered in brown paper – assemble one entire 9 x 9in (23 x 23cm) cake and butt one of the half pieces you have set aside up to it. Cover this in chocolate butter icing so that you have a 13½ x 9in, chocolate-covered, cake. Make sure that the icing covers all the sides as well as an area 2½ inches in front of one of the long sides of the fort, which will be the stockade.

Divide the piece you have set aside into eight smaller pieces. Sandwich these together with butter icing to give you four taller pieces. Trim the corners of the rectangular central cake and place one of these pieces at each corner to make the 'lookout towers' of the fort. Cover them in butter icing so that they attach and become one with the central fort.

Place a small flag, made out of a cocktail stick and paper, on top of each tower. Link the towers by carefully sticking small pieces of chocolate fingers, or chocolate buttons, side by side, into the icing along the top edges of the main 'fort', to make low walls, running between the towers. If you have a few small cowboy figures, or medieval knights, place them on guard behind these walls.

Now make the walls of the stockade, out of sponge fingers. Cut each biscuit in half and arrange side by side in front of the fort, planting them in the butter icing. Leave a gap for the gate. Make the gate out of a rectangular chocolate biscuit.

Paint the brown paper at the base of the fort with a little beaten white of egg and scatter brown sugar on it, as 'desert sand'.

Number Cake, or Clock Cake

Victoria sponge (to fit size of your number or letter mould)
Chocolate cream filling
Butter icing
Chocolate Fingers
Smarties

You can buy or hire 'number' tins, but some numbers are fairly simple to construct yourself – numbers 1,3,7 and 10 can all be made using either ring moulds or round, loaf-shaped, or square baking tins and carving pieces with a very sharp knife. Ice the finished 'numbers' with butter icing which is good for covering up mistakes and for holding separate pieces of cake together.

To make a Clock Cake, bake 2 x 7in plain sponges (see Victoria sponge recipe above). Sandwich them together with chocolate cream filling. Cover with butter icing. This should be in a light colour so that the clock 'hands', which you can make out of chocolate fingers, will stand out. For the numbers, arrange 12 smarties around the edge of the cake, in positions 1 to 12 o'clock. Set the hands at the age of the birthday boy or girl.

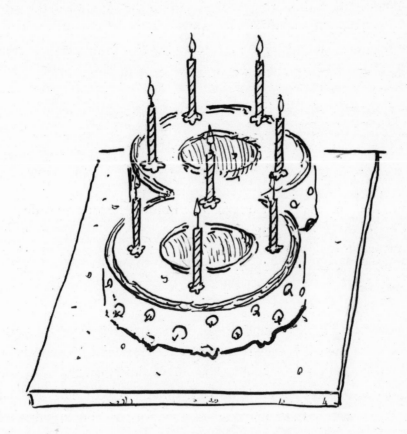

Happy Birthday Cupcakes

Victoria sponge mixture, using 3 eggs (for 12 cupcakes)
Apricot glaze
Glacé icing

This is a very simple variation on the normal cake theme, which goes down very well at parties. The idea is to provide an individual cupcake, rather than a slice of cake, for each guest at the party. You can arrange the cupcakes however you want, sticking a single candle in each of a central group of cakes according to the age of the child. So, if you are doing a sixth birthday party with 12 guests, you might arrange 12 cupcakes on a large round plate, with candles in the six cakes at the centre.

Make the cupcakes using the recipe for Victoria sponge on page 134, and bake them in paper muffin cases. When they are cool, spread with warm apricot glaze. Then spread with warm pink or chocolate glacé icing. You can decorate the cakes now as you want. If you are a dab hand at piping, you can, for example, pipe the number of the child's age in fine white glacé icing on top of all the cakes. Alternatively, you can pipe a letter on each cake to make your grandchild's name.

Crinoline Lady

This cake is taken from *Children's Parties*, by Angela Hollest and Penelope Graine, lent to me by the sister-in-law of a friend, whose children are grown up and probably masters of the universe by now. It is a wonderfully Eighties book, with children in smocked lawn dresses, pie-frilled collars on the mums and even a party game called 'Prince Charles, Princess Diana and their carriage'.

Madeira sponge (quantities as for 9in square tin above)
A Barbie or similar doll, about 9in/23cm high
Butter icing
A little marzipan
Silver balls
Pink icing flowers

Make the Madeira sponge mixture and bake for about 1hr 30 mins in a greased 2 pint/1.1 litre ovenproof bowl of the kind used for steaming Christmas puddings, or a Pyrex bowl. Test with a skewer after 1 hour.

Meanwhile take a Barbie, dressed from the waist up, in a simple strapless bandeau. Remove her legs! (This sounds alarming, but most Barbie dolls have legs that pop in and pop out with ease...) The cake will form the crinoline skirt.

If necessary trim the cake to make it level, and turn it out on to a board or large plate.

Make butter icing and ice the cake, spreading it on with a palette knife. Make crinoline panniers by setting three rows of tiny silver balls in loops a small distance apart around the top of the 'skirt'. Arrange some pink icing flowers at the base of the skirt and more at the loops of the swags. Now press the doll into the cake and use the last of the butter icing with some tiny silver balls to taper the skirt into her 'waist'.

Pirate Treasure Chest

Pirate parties are all the rage among 5- to 7-year-olds, and this cake would be perfect.

Madeira sponge, amounts as for two 9 x 9in squares
Chocolate glacé or chocolate butter icing
Sweets: maltesers, smarties, haribos, jelly tots, etc
A little jam
Readymade decorative black icing

Make Madeira mixture and divide into two large bread tins (9 x 4 x 4in/23 x 10 x 10cm) in two unequal parts, approximately one to two thirds. The larger of the baked cakes is going to provide the base of the chest, while the smaller one is going to be chiselled into a curved lid.

For the lower part of the chest: using a sharp knife, cut a rectangular slab out of the upper centre of the large cake, making a hole and leaving about an inch and a half of cake on the base and sides, to look like the bottom of a treasure chest. Put this gouged-out piece on a cakeboard, and fill it with sweets: maltezers, smarties, haribos, jelly tots, gold coins…

For the lid: place your second slab of cake on a board in front of you. Carefully cut and chisel away at the sides and corners of the block to make a curved chest lid which fits nicely on top of your base. You want this piece to be one third of the height of the base chest piece at its highest. Cover the entire chest with chocolate glace or chocolate butter icing, and leave to set.

Using a tube of readymade decorative black icing, squirt lines up and over the top of the chest, to make it look as if it is made from planks of wood. From a packet of haribos, take one of the keyhole-shaped sweets and stick it on to the front of the lower part of the chest using some jam. Make a Jolly Roger skull and cross-bone flag, fix it to a cocktail stick and stick it beside the chest in a fragment of cake, iced to look like a rock.

Arrange the candles along the top ridge of your treasure chest. And ensure that the birthday boy or girl makes the first cut, to let all the sweets tumble out!

Bunny Cake

7in round chocolate sponge
Sponge fingers
Chocolate butter icing
Readymade icing
Chocolate buttons
A red M&M
A pink/strawberry liquorice bootlace

This is an extremely simple cake to make, and always much loved by little ones.

Bake a chocolate sponge according to the Victoria sponge recipe on page 134. Turn it out and place it on wire rack until cool. This is the bunny's head.

Take two sponge fingers and chop a matching small amount off one end of each and place them in the ear position.

Cover everything with chocolate butter icing.

For the eyes, make two round circles out of white readymade icing and put a chocolate button in the centre of each.

Use a red M&M for the nose and make the mouth out of a bit of pink liquorice bootlace. To make the whiskers, cut out thin strips of more readymade white icing, and arrange them, coming out cartoon-style, from the mouth.

Hansel and Gretel Cottage

Two 9 x 9in Madeira cakes
Chocolate butter icing
White glacé icing
Sweets: chocolate buttons, smarties, jelly tots, etc
Chocolate finger biscuits
Hundreds and Thousands

A friend of mine, who used this recipe in a last-minute dash for her granddaughter's fourth birthday, said she was extremely proud of her charmingly naïve cake, but that it turned out to be more a 'Hansel and Gretel barn with subsidence' than a cottage.

Cut both of the 9in Madeira cakes into two slabs, one of six inches wide and one of three inches. Take the two larger slabs, of 6 x 9in each, and sandwich them one on top of one another with chocolate butter icing. This is the body of the cottage.

Next take each of the smaller, 3 x 9in slabs, and divide them diagonally, lengthways. Choose the two most evenly matched pieces (using slices from the two discarded pieces to patch up any dips or holes!), and stick them side by side on top of the cottage with butter icing, to make a long, gabled roof. Cover the entire cottage with chocolate butter icing.

Stick rows of chocolate buttons into the icing on the roof as tiles. Use very stiff white glacé icing to pipe window and door frames. Using jam, stick on two bourbon biscuits for the door, and jelly tots or smarties all over the walls as stones or bricks. You can then make a garden: spread butter icing on the board around the house, and stick colourful sweets into it for flowers, use hundreds and thousands to make a gravel pathway, and chocolate fingers for the garden fence.

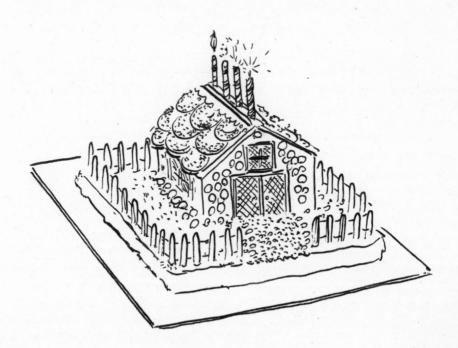

Hedgehog Cake

Victoria sponge mixture using 4 eggs
Chocolate butter icing
Chocolate cream filling
2 large packets of chocolate buttons
Silver balls
A glacé cherry

Make a Victoria sponge mixture using 4 eggs, pour into a greased and floured 10 in/24cm diameter Pyrex pudding basin, and bake for about an hour.

Test with a skewer to see that the cake is cooked in the centre. When cool, turn the cake out. Cut it in half horizontally and sandwich with chocolate cream filling.

Spread chocolate butter icing all over the cake and lift it on to a plate or cake board. Put a little extra icing at one end and form this into a point for the 'snout'.

Place chocolate buttons into the butter icing at an angle, covering the entire cake, except the front quarter.

Make sure the button points all face in the same direction, as they represent spines. Mark the face with a fork and put a glace cherry on the end of the snout.

Use two silver balls for the eyes.

Winter Wonderland Cake

Two 9 x 9in Madeira cakes
A frameless pocket mirror about 4 x 3in (can be bought from
    most chemists)
Pure white butter icing
Cake 'frill' in silver
Miniature Christmas trees and a tiny sledge
Silver balls

My birthday is in February and I always thought I missed out compared to my brother and cousins with summer birthdays. A cake like this would certainly have made up for it.

Line the Madeira cakes up side-by-side on a foil-covered board and cut 3 inches off one end to leave a 9 x 15in cake. Put the pocket mirror on the cake, slightly to one end. Cover the cake in white butter icing, bringing it just over the edge of the glass to give a 'lake' effect.

Cut out a cake 'frill' in silver or silver and white and pin around the edge of the cake. Arrange miniature Christmas trees and a tiny sledge on the cake. At the clearer end write the child's name in silver balls.

♣ 4 ♣

Great Days Out with Granny

Once in a while, you'll want to take your grandchildren on a really memorable outing. It could include the whole family, but you may like to give one child his or her own special treat, just the two of you. Well, perhaps Grandpa too.

To be sure your grandchildren have a really good time, it's worth tailoring the day to their interests. At different times they may be keen on the Romans, medieval knights, dinosaurs, giraffes or Thomas (Thomas who? Thomas the Tank Engine, of course). The right choice of venue might help them with a school project, too. The lists that follow offer something for everyone.

There are a few general principles to ensure a good time is had by all:

∘ If you possibly can, avoid half term and Bank Holiday weekends. If you are treating pre-school age children, take them in term time.

∘ Aim to get there at opening time or soon after, or go towards the end of the day. These are usually the least busy times.

∘ Check opening times and work out how to get there. Download from the Internet a map of your route – one copy for each child – and let them follow it in the car.

° Brush up your car games to make the journey go quickly (see the list at the end of the chapter).

° Don't try and do everything. At places where there are multiple attractions, pick the three or four that most appeal to your group and stick to them. You can always come again next year.

° A picnic is often more fun for children than lunch in a café or restaurant. They can run about instead of having to queue at a cafeteria or sit at a table waiting to be served. It's easier on Granny's pocket too. But check the weather forecast. It's not much fun picnicking in the car.

° Build little rests into the day, when Granny can take the weight off her feet. It might be a pause for an ice cream or drink, or, where such things are not available, a drink and snack conjured out of Granny's capacious bag.

° Unless you actually want to buy the children presents, steer clear of the souvenir shop. Just tell them you haven't got any money; then there can be no argument.

Castles, Palaces and Forts

BODIAM CASTLE
Bodiam, Nr Robertsbridge, East Sussex, TN32 5UA (01580 830196) www.nationaltrust.org.uk/places/bodiamcastle
A perfect, medieval moated castle. There are battlements to explore and armour can sometimes be tried on.

CAWDOR CASTLE

Cawdor, Nairn, Scotland, IV12 5RD (01667 404401) www.cawdor-castle.com

Famous as Macbeth's castle when he fulfilled the three witches' prophecy that he would become Thane of Cawdor. There's a large old yew maze and Cawdor Big Wood, with its ancient trees and occasional red deer, is perfect for exploring.

FORT NELSON: THE ROYAL ARMOURIES

Portsdown Hill Road, Fareham, Hampshire, PO17 6AN (01329 233734) www.armouries.org.uk

Take them to see the 'Boxted Bombard', an English cannon from around 1450, which was powerful enough to fire a 60kg granite ball. They can learn how soldiers lived in the bad old days and explore tunnels below this 19th-century fort, built to defend us against the French.

HAMPTON COURT, THE THAMES

East Molesley, Surrey, KT8 9AU (0844 482 7777) www.hrp.org.uk

A spectacular palace, great for a whole day out, with stunning gardens, particularly beautiful in spring. There are excellent events and demonstrations, to show children what life was like in Henry VIII's time. To add to the experience you can arrive by boat from Kew, as King Henry would have done.

HAMPTON COURT, HEREFORDSHIRE

Hope Under Dinmore, Herefordshire, HR6 0PN (01568 797 777) www.hamptoncourt.org.uk

The other Hampton Court is less crowded, with vast lawns, a very smart café and a maze of a thousand yews with a gothic tower at its centre. Race your grandchildren to the top (not too many steps) for a panoramic view of the gardens.

HEVER CASTLE
Hever, Nr Edenbridge, Kent, TN8 7NG (01732 865 224)
www.hevercastle.co.uk
Take a picnic to eat in the wonderful surroundings of Anne Boleyn's childhood home. There's a water maze and boating on the lake between Easter and October.

LEEDS CASTLE
Maidstone, Kent, ME17 1PL (01622 765400) www.leeds-castle.com
A fairytale castle on a river, with wonderful grounds. For older children there are model towers to climb, secret tunnels and rope bridges in the huge, well designed adventure playground. There is also an aviary and opportunities to watch falcons and birds of prey at work.

TOWER OF LONDON
London, EC3N 4AB (0844 482 7777) www.hrp.org.uk
See the White Tower, the Crown Jewels and the Yeoman Warders. The Bloody Tower is so called because of the number of executions that took place there. You can also see where the Princes in the Tower were imprisoned, Tower Green where Anne Boleyn was executed, and the spot where an attempt was made to steal the Crown Jewels. Of Henry VIII's wives three were beheaded, including poor Anne:

Divorced, beheaded, died, divorced, beheaded, survived

WARWICK CASTLE

Warwick, Warwickshire, CV34 4QU (08704 422 000)
www.warwick-castle.co.uk

A magnificent medieval castle with every imaginable entertainment – ranging from a ghost tower and jousting tournaments, to an interactive battle sequence, as seen through the eyes of a 12-year-old soldier, going into battle for the Earl of Warwick. There is a large park, and plenty of play areas.

Zoos and Wildlife Parks

Most children are fascinated by exotic animals and enjoy visiting them in zoos and wildlife parks. Some adults, on the other hand, are uneasy about animals being reared in captivity, and feel it is unethical. However, many zoos do invaluable work looking after rare or endangered species.

Some animals are just too big for small children to comprehend. When my grandchildren were toddlers, they were completely unimpressed by elephants.

BEALE PARK

The Child-Beale Trust, Lower Basildon, Reading,
Berkshire, RG8 9NH (0870 7777160) www.bealepark.co.uk

You can walk through an aviary, along nature trails, past an owlery and through a small deer park, all on the banks of the Thames, with summer river cruises, adventure playgrounds, paddling pools and a miniature railway.

BELFAST ZOO
**Bellevue, Antrim Road, Newtown Abbey, BT36 7PN,
Northern Ireland (028 9077 6277) www.belfastzoo.co.uk**
The zoo's 55-acre site in North Belfast is home to more than 1,200 animals and 140 species, including white tigers, Barbary lions, elephants, giraffes and gorillas. The biggest attraction is Lily, a Barbary lion cub, born in June 2007, weighing only 1.4kg and measuring just 37cm. Barbary lions are extinct in the wild, and zoos are the only hope for their survival.

BLACKPOOL ZOO
**East Park Dr, Blackpool, FY3 8PP (01253 830830)
www.blackpoolzoo.org.uk**
Two miles from the sea-front, set in 32 acres of lake-filled parkland, there are 1,500 animals including lions, tigers and Asian elephants.

BRISTOL ZOO GARDENS
Clifton, Bristol, BS8 3HA, (0117 974 7399) www.bristolzoo.org
The fifth oldest zoo in the world and the oldest outside a capital city is set in outstanding gardens and some of the animal houses are listed buildings. It has the world's first Twilight Zone for marsupials, as well as insect and reptile houses, an aquarium, several aviaries and a seal and penguin enclosure. There are also gorillas, monkeys, lemurs, pelicans and a stunning under-water view of sea-lions swimming. Also a good adventure playground.

CHESTER ZOO
Caughall Rd, Upton, Chester, CH2 1LH, (01244 380280)
www.chesterzoo.org

> *A rare old bird is the Pelican,*
> *His beak can hold more than his belly can.*
> *He can hold in his beak enough food for a week.*
> *I'm damned if I see how the hell he can.*

In over 100 acres, close to the city of Chester, this zoo has over 7,000 animals and more than 400 species of rare, exotic and endangered wildlife. There is a play park and award-winning gardens.

COTSWOLD WILDLIFE PARK
Cotswold Wildlife Park, Burford, Oxfordshire, OX18 4JP
(01993 823006) www.cotswoldwildlifepark.co.uk
There are rhinos and camels, flamingos, meerkats and a green anaconda and beautifully maintained gardens, including a water garden with giant lily pads, and woods where children can literally feed the tree ferns with bananas. This is my local, where the Thomas the Tank Engine train was as much of a draw as the animals when my grandchildren were little.

Tip: On chilly days you can warm up in the reptile house where the temperature is kept consistently high.

CRICKET ST THOMAS
Chard, Somerset, TA20 4DB (01460 30111) www.cstwp.co.uk
The lemurs, meerkats and flamingos were voted favourite creatures

when we visited this park. The safari train goes past some puppet tableaux which are slightly scary for the smallest children.

DRUSILLA'S PARK
Alfriston, Lewes, East Sussex, BN26 5QS (01323 874 100)
www.drusillas.co.uk
A small established zoo, with some nice, old-fashioned rides, which, if they can't compete with the best of modern attractions, have a certain faded charm. A Thomas the Tank engine train goes around the grounds. There is a popular attraction where children can see how fast they can run (about 40 kph) and how loud they can scream (about 110 decibels) and then compare their achievements to various types of animal. There's also a 'keeper for a day' scheme.

EDINBURGH ZOO
134 Corstorphine Road, Edinburgh, EH12 6TS (0131 334 9171)
www.edinburghzoo.org.uk
This zoo on the outskirts of Edinburgh has the world's largest chimpanzee enclosure, the Budongo Trail, with as many as 40 chimpanzees. It's also the only zoo in Britain to have polar bears and koalas.

HOWLETT'S AND PORT LYMPNE
Both parks were started by John Aspinall with the aim of protecting and breeding rare and endangered species and returning them to safe areas in their native lands. So far, the parks have returned to the wild Przewalski's horses, black rhino, Sumatran rhino, Cape buffalo, ocelots, pythons and gorillas.

Howletts

Bekesbourne, Canterbury, Kent (01227 721286)
www.howletts.net

This, the smaller park, is set in 90 acres near Canterbury. A 90-minute ride on the park's safari 4x4 shows you the largest group of western lowland gorillas in captivity in the world and the largest herd of African elephants in the UK. Also tigers, monkeys, small cats, bongo, tapirs and wolves.

Port Lympne (near Hythe)

Port Lympne Wild Animal Park, Lympne, Nr Hythe, Kent (01303 264647) www.howletts.net

In 400 acres of open country, the safari trail here passes among the largest herd of captive-bred black rhinos outside Africa. There are Indian elephants, Siberian and Indian tigers, Barbary lions, and the world's largest gorillarium: the Palace of the Apes. The great Edwardian house and its spectacular formal gardens were restored by John Aspinall.

KNOWSLEY SAFARI PARK

Prescot, Merseyside (0151 430 9009) www.knowsley.com
Set in 550 acres of the Earl of Derby's Estate, the park features a five-mile safari drive. There is a strong educational programme. Play facilities include Jungle Dodgems, a traditional Carousel and a Pirate Ship.

LONDON ZOO

Regent's Park, London, NW1 4RY (020 7722 3333) www.zsl.org
The daddy of all zoos is now devoted to conservation. When it's cold outside, take them to virtual South America in the new jungle aviary, filled with tropical trees and alive with South American monkeys, birds and invertebrates. Altogether there are about 700 species in the zoo, although the larger animals – elephants and rhinos – are now at Whipsnade where they have more space.

LONGLEAT

Warminster, Wiltshire, BA12 7NW (01985 844 400) www.longleat. co.uk
The Marquess of Bath opened Britain's first safari park in 1966. Allow a full day to see everything, and take a picnic (a friend who went

recently said she could recommend neither the food in the restaurant, nor its prices). If the children tire of driving past lions, tigers, rhinos, zebras and giraffes, there are mazes, adventure castles, a pets' corner, safari boats and a miniature railway. Children (but not grown-ups) love driving through the monkey enclosure; monkeys swarm all over the car and you risk car trimmings being torn off.

MONKEY FOREST
Trentham Estate, Southern Entrance, Stone Rd, Stoke-on-Trent, Staffordshire, ST4 8AX (01782 657341) www.monkey-forest.com
At Trentham Gardens they are strong on conservation, with a colony of almost 150 captive-bred Barbary macaque apes living semi-wild. There is a boating lake with catamaran rides and an adventure park with rope and aerial rides for older grandchildren.

PAIGNTON ZOO
Paignton, Devon (01803 697500) www.paigntonzoo.org.uk
Thousands of animals in 80 acres of natural habitat. Also a miniature train and wobbly jungle bridge.

THRIGBY HALL WILDLIFE GARDENS
Filby, Gt Yarmouth, Norfolk, NR29 3DR, (01493 369477)
www.thrigby.plus.com
A charming small zoo with Chinese pavilions, a tree walk and a great reptile house. Generally praised, although one visitor said loos could be cleaner. There's a tiger tree walk, an award-winning enclosure for crocodiles and alligators, and the grounds include a Willow Pattern Garden.

Two little birds, flying high,
Sailing vessel passing by,
Little bridge with willows o'er,
Three men on it if not four.
Orange tree with oranges on
And little wooden fence all along.

TWYCROSS ZOO
Burton Road, Atherstone, Warwickshire, Leicestershire, CV9 3PX
(01827 880250) www.twycrosszoo.com
Home to a collection of primates roaming through 40 acres of open
countryside. Other animals include lemurs and giraffes. About
three quarters of the animals are from endangered species, and
there is an education programme. Also a play area with a pirates'
cove.

WELSH MOUNTAIN ZOO
Old Highway, Colwyn Bay, Colwyn, LL28 5UY (01492 32938)
www.welshmountainzoo.org
In North Wales, high above Colwyn Bay, this conservation zoo con-
tains rare and endangered species from Britain and around the world,
including snow leopards, chimpanzees, red pandas and Sumatran tigers. There is a Penguin Parade, a Chimp Encounter, Bear Falls, Con-
dor Haven and a children's farm. There are also sea lions, a jungle
adventure land and a Tarzan Trail adventure playground.

WEST MIDLANDS SAFARI AND LEISURE PARK
Spring Grove, Bewdley, Worcestershire, DY12 1LF (01299 402114)
www.wmsp.co.uk
The four-mile drive features, among other animals, two cheetahs –
the fastest animals on earth – and a family of rare white lions.

WHIPSNADE WILD ANIMAL PARK
Dunstable, Bedfordshire, LU6 2LF (01582 872 171) www.zsl.org
Whipsnade, a branch of London Zoo, is home to over 2,500 wild
animals. Look for the white lion carved into Dunstable Downs below
the penguin enclosure. Once in the park, you can walk, use the zoo's
bus service, or drive your car between the various enclosures. There
is also a narrow gauge train, the Jumbo Express. Most animals live in
large enclosures; others, such as the peacocks, the South American
Mara and Australian wallabies, roam freely around the park.

WOBURN SAFARI PARK
Milton Keynes, Bedfordshire, MK17 9QN (01525 290407)
www.woburnsafari.co.uk
You can combine a safari drive through the park with a foot expe-
dition to meet animals on a more personal level in the Wild World
leisure centre; there are keeper talks and animal demos.

Fantastic Farms

If you live in the country, look out for open days at local farms,
specially in the spring at lambing time.

CHATSWORTH
Bakewell, Derbyshire, DE45 1PP (01246 565300)
www.chatsworth.org
The Duke and Duchess of Devonshire's Chatsworth is one of the grandest of all stately homes and estates. The farmyard is just one of many things to see and explore: there are piglets, goats and many other animals, milking demonstrations and animal handling sessions. Also a maze, a woodland adventure playground, water play and spiral slides – something for every child. In the gardens, look for the famous stepped water cascade and the joke willow tree fountain.

CORAM'S FIELDS
Guilford Street, Camden, London, WC1N 1DN (0207 837 6138)
www.ocrmansfields.org
Bang in the middle of the city centre are five acres of park, a playground and a small farm with goats, sheep, pigs and rabbits. Thomas Coram was an 18th-century philanthropist who set up a Foundling Hospital on the site. Adults are only allowed in if accompanied by a child. Children can splash in the paddling pool, swing on the climbing frame and play in the huge sandpit.

COTSWOLD FARM PARK
Guiting Power, Gloucestershire (01451 850 30) www.cotswold-farmpark.co.uk
A fun day out regardless of the weather. Children can meet, cuddle and feed a variety of farm animals. The park is also home to rare breeds of sheep, cattle, pigs, goats and waterfowl.

FREIGHTLINERS CITY FARM

Sheringham Road, London, N7 8PF (0207 609 0467)
www.freightlinersfarm.org.uk

An inner-city working farm, which puts on special activities for under-fives twice a week.

MARSH FARM COUNTRY PARK

Marsh Farm Road, South Woodham Ferrers, Essex, CM3 5WP
(01245 321552) www.marshfarm.co.uk

A working farm where children can get close to farm animals and play safely in the adventure play areas. There is also a country park, with coastal walks. Seasonal activities and events throughout the year.

NOAH'S ARK ZOO FARM

Failand Road, Wraxall, Bristol, North Somerset, BS48 1PG
(01275 852606) www.noahsarkzoofarm.co.uk

Set in beautiful countryside, with a view across the river Severn to South Wales, this zoo farm has a huge range of animals, from rhinos, camels, monkeys and meerkats to baby chicks, lambs, rabbits and guinea pigs. There are large indoor and outdoor adventure playgrounds, with soft play areas for toddlers; the World's Longest Hedge Maze, planted in 2003; and an indoor 3D 'Beehive' Maze which has been built on five floors. Take a picnic.

ODDS FARM PARK

Wooburn Common Road, Wooburn Common, High Wycombe,
Bucks, HP10 0LX (01628 520188) www.oddsfarm.co.uk

An intimate and user-friendly park, where visitors can get close to the animals. Great for young ones.

REDE HALL FARM PARK
**Rede Hall Farm Park, Rede, Bury St. Edmunds, Suffolk, IP29 4UG
(01284 8506950) www.redehallfarmpark.co.uk**
This farm offers children 'hands on' experience with the animals.
There is a working blacksmith (ring first to check which days he is
there), and a yard where old farm machinery is restored; free cart
and pony rides and a nice picnic area.

WHITE POST FARM CENTRE
**Farnsfield, Newark, Nottinghamshire, NG22 8HL (01623 882977)
www.whitepostfarmcentre.co.uk**
There are animals including reptiles, llamas and bats. Other activities include an outdoor play area with forts, trampolines, and pedal
go-karts and an indoor play barn with a large indoor sledge run, sand
and mini tractors. For smaller children, there is also an indoor soft
play area.

Amazing Mazes

Mazes excite children of all ages, their enjoyment being spiced with
a frisson of fear that they just might never find the way out. Send the
children into the maze, find yourself somewhere comfortable to sit,
and shut your eyes (just for a moment). If you can't make it to one of
the historic mazes mentioned here, look out for maize mazes in the
summer, at a farm near you.

ALICE IN WONDERLAND FAMILY PARK

Merritown Lane, Christchurch, Dorset, BH23 6BA (01202 483444) www.aliceinwonderlandpark.co.uk

The Alice Maze is one of the largest in the country. The seven-acre park also has rides, astroslide, bouncy castle, swingboats, farm animals, and a soft play area. Alice, the Mad Hatter, the Queen of Hearts and the White Rabbit welcome you to the park, and every day the characters have a storytelling in the Alice Theatre, based on stories from Lewis Carroll's Alice books.

BLENHEIM PALACE

Woodstock, Oxfordshire, OX20 1PX (08700 60 20 80) www.blenheimpalace.com

There is much to see and do here but, for children, the Marlborough Maze is a highlight. The world's second largest symbolic hedge maze, designed to reflect the history and architecture of the Palace, it covers just over an acre. Two high wooden bridges provide vantage points. Within the maze area, there is a model of a Woodstock street, putting greens, and a giant chess and draughts set.

CASTLE BROMWICH

Chester Road, Castle Bromwich, Birmingham, B36 9BT (0121 749 4100) www.cbhtg.org.uk

The Holly Maze is a distorted mirror image of the maze at Hampton Court Palace, designed by George London and Henry Wise.

GLENDURGAN HOUSE

Nr Falmouth, Cornwall (01872 862090) www.nationaltrust.org.uk

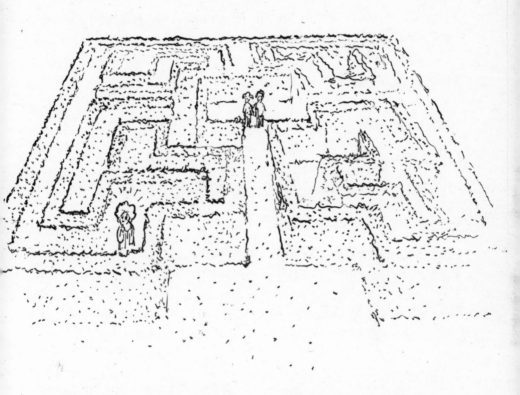

A superb subtropical garden and beautifully restored 19th-century laurel maze.

SCONE PALACE
Perth, Scotland (01738 552300) www.scone-palace.net
The new Murray Star Maze here was designed by international maze designer, Adrian Fisher, to reflect the history of the Murray family.

TATTON PARK

Knutsford, Cheshire, WA16 6QN (01625 374435) www.tattonpark. org.uk

The maze is just one feature in 50 acres of fine historic gardens, known especially for rhododendrons and azaleas.

More mazes at:

BEKONSCOT See *Railways*, below.

CAWDOR CASTLE See *Castles*, above.

EDINBURGH ZOO See *Zoos & Wildlife Parks*, above.

LONGLEAT Five in all – see *Zoos & Wildlife Parks*, above.

HAMPTON COURT Both on the Thames and in Herefordshire. See *Palaces*, above.

HEVER CASTLE A water maze: you follow the stepping stones to try to reach the island in the lake without getting soaked. See *Castles*, above.

LEEDS CASTLE Two mazes: a traditional hedge maze and a turf maze for under fives in their own play area. See *Castles*, above.

LEGOLAND See *Very Special Treats*, below.

Adventure Playgrounds

ALNWICK GARDEN
Alnwick Castle, Denwick Lane, Alnwick, NE66 1NQ (01665 511350) www.alnwickcastle.com
Controversial (because of their huge cost) but stunning gardens made in the last ten years in the grounds of a Northumberland castle. Children can explore an enormous tree house with its suspended walkways and wobbly rope bridge. It's a great garden for getting wet in, so bring a change of clothes for the children. Other attractions include a poison garden where you can discover gruesome facts about nasty plants. Eat in the family Tree House restaurant or take a picnic.

BELTON HOUSE
Grantham, Lincolnshire, NG32 2LS (01476 566116) www.nationaltrust.org.uk
This magnificent 17th-century country house has been a film location for the BBC's *Jane Eyre* and *Pride and Prejudice*. It also boasts the National Trust's largest adventure playground.

BEWILDERWOOD
Horning Road, Hoveton, Wroxham, Norwich, NR12 8JW (0870 0130705)
This rural theme park, just north of Norwich, has 50 eco-friendly acres of tree houses, mazes and zip wires – described by its creator, Tom Blofeld, as 'a reality adventure for bold and daring children'. Under-fives have their own entrance through the Twiggle Door

leading to colourful houses, a roly-poly hill, swings and a climbing course.

BOWOOD HOUSE
Calne, Wiltshire, SN11 OLZ (01249 812102) www.bowood-house. co.uk

There is more than enough at Bowood to fill a whole day. The adventure playground has a full-size pirate galleon, some very large slides, and high-level walkways reached via a huge scramble net. For the most intrepid, the 'death slide' has a 19-foot vertical drop that levels out into a fast and slippery slide. For younger children there are swing boats, trampolines, a Wendy House, and a sand pit. Granny will want to look round the house, and can lure the children inside with a promise to see the tigerskin rug in the library. Take a picnic, and wander through the park to a grotto and waterfall where you can walk through a tunnel in the rocks (test it for echoes).

Into the Jungle

THE EDEN PROJECT
Bodelva, St Austell, Cornwall, PL24 2SG (01726 811911) www. edenproject.com

Created on the site of abandoned china clay pits, the Eden Project has become a major tourist attraction in Cornwall. A series of giant, 21st-century greenhouses or biomes – including one tropical and one Mediterranean – house over 100,000 plants, representing 5,000 species from different climate zones of the world.

GLASGOW BOTANIC GARDENS
730 Great Western Road, Glasgow, G12 OUE (0141 334 3354)
www.glasgow.gov.uk
To escape winter, wander through some of the 11 Victorian glass-houses here. The children can pretend they are in steaming Amazonia. See the eye-catching orchids of the forest canopy, then move into the immense palm house for an insect's-eye view of sunlight filtering down through a tangle of lianas and bananas. In the tropical pond house, there are water lilies as big as your head.

ROYAL BOTANIC GARDENS, KEW
Richmond, Surrey, TW9 3AB (020 8332 5655) www.kew.org
In the glass-covered Temperate House and Palm House, aerial walkways give a new perspective on the plants. You can climb to the tree-tops on walkways 18 metres high, and see the world's largest indoor plant, the Chilean wine-palm (*Jubaea chilensis*), in the centre of the Temperate House; it's 16m (52ft) high and still growing. You can arrive at Kew by Thames riverboat and, if it's too hot in the jungle, young children will enjoy the Badger's Sett and the Climbers and Creepers playground. Plenty to keep them happy all day long.

Ancient Britain

AVEBURY STONE CIRCLE
Nr Marlborough, Wiltshire, SN8 1RF (01672 539250)
www.nationaltrust.org.uk
A World Heritage Site – one of Europe's largest prehistoric stone

circles, at the heart of a prehistoric landscape. It's as mysterious and awe-inspiring as Stonehenge, and has the advantage of free (in every sense) access. Families can walk among the stones and touch them, and children can let off steam running about and rolling down steep grassy banks. Archaeological finds are displayed in an on-site museum.

HADRIAN'S WALL
(01434 322002) www.hadrians-wall.org
Hadrian's Wall forms a 73-mile barrier stretching from the River Tyne in the east to the Solway Firth in the west. One of the best introductions to life in the Roman army is to visit Segedunum, which means 'strong fort'. Now a World Heritage Site, it is at the eastern end of the Wall and was home to 600 Roman soldiers, who guarded this important part of the frontier. It is the most excavated fort along the Wall and has a large interactive museum and a 35m high viewing tower.

JORVIK VIKING CENTRE
Coppergate, York, YO1 9WT (01904 643 211)
www.Jorvik-viking-centre.co.uk
On this site the York Archaeological Trust discovered perfectly preserved remains of Viking York (Jorvik) encased in wet mud. The centre re-creates this world through a series of tableaux depicting markets, shops, street scenes, and other aspects of daily life.

ROMAN BATHS
The Roman Baths, Pump Room, Stall Street, Bath, BA1 1LZ

(01225 477 785) www.romanbaths.co.uk
Britain's only hot spring, where the Romans built a temple and baths
and fashionable Georgian society came to take the waters. Children
can walk on ancient stone pavements where Romans once walked.
They may meet Peregrinus Sulimus, a local sculptor, and his stone-
mason father, Brucetus, or Flavia and her servant, Apulia. Close by is
the Pump Room where you can drink mineral water for your health.
It tastes of bad eggs. Also in Bath are the Assembly Rooms where
Jane Austen's heroines danced, and an excellent costume museum.

Let off Steam on Some Railway Rides

For young addicts any train journey is a treat easily provided by going one or two stops from your local station to a different park or
a change of shopping centre. But nothing beats a steam engine for
sheer romance, whatever your age.

BEKONSCOT MODEL VILLAGE AND RAILWAY
**Warwick Road, Beaconsfield, Buckinghamshire, HP9 2PL (01494
672919) www.bekonscot.com**
Paradise for model railway addicts. With over 400 metres of realis-
tically-signalled main line and branch line, there are normally between seven and ten trains running at any one time. The village and
its gardens are perfectly to scale. Children love it and grandparents
relish the snapshot it gives of life in 1930s Britain (before grannies
were born).

THE BLUEBELL LINE
Sheffield Park Station, East Sussex, TN22 3QL (01825 722370)
www.bluebell-railway.co.uk
The UK's first preserved standard gauge passenger railway now carries passengers from Sheffield Park to Kingscote and back. Almost every time you see an old steam train sequence in an English film it will have been shot on the Bluebell line.

DRAYTON MANOR THEME PARK
Near Tamworth, Staffordshire, B78 3TW, (0844 4721960)
www.draytonmanor.co.uk
Thomas Land is a part of the theme park, specially for younger children with their very own rollercoaster, vertical drop, a Thomas the Tank Engine ride and Terence the Tractors mini-tractors driving school. It's brand new, and the only other one is in Japan.

THE SWANAGE RAILWAY
The Square, Corfe Castle, Wareham, Dorset, BH20 5EZ
(01929 481294)   www.swanagerailway.co.uk
Take the train from Swanage to Corfe Castle, where the children can explore the ruins, roll down the grassy slopes and re-enact battles between knights. Enid Blyton fans may recognise Corfe Castle as the inspiration behind Kirrin Castle in the 'Famous Five' series.

THE TALYLLYN RAILWAY
Talyllyn Railway Company, Wharf Station, Tywyn, Gwynedd,
Wales, LL36 9EY www.talyllyn.co.uk
We took our children and their friends on this train nearly 40 years ago, as a change from the beach at Aberdovey, and they loved it,

so it's good to know it's still going strong. It's a historic narrow-gauge steam railway, set in beautiful mid-Wales countryside. The line runs from Tywyn to Abergynolwyn and Nant Gwernol, passing the Dolgoch Falls, and there are lovely forest walks at Nant Gwernol.

THOMAS & FRIENDS AT THE DEAN FOREST RAILWAY
Dean Forest Railway, Norchard, Forest Road, Lydney, Gloucester-shire, GL15 4ET (01594 845840), www.deanforestrailway.co.uk
Thomas the Tank Engine makes a guest appearance here just a few times each year. Children get to meet the Fat Controller and under-sixes have a delirious time. Granny gets exhausted – to reach Thomas you run the gamut of candy floss, hot dog, ice-cream and souvenir stalls, and it's so crowded that you go in mortal fear of losing a child. But the children's delight makes it all worth while. Book tickets in advance to save queuing. Take a picnic.

WELSHPOOL & LLANFAIR LIGHT RAILWAY PRESERVATION CO. LIMITED,
The Station, Llanfair, Caereinion, Welshpool, Powys, SY21 0SF (01938 810441) info@wllr.org.uk
A 16-mile return journey by narrow gauge steam train through un-spoilt mid-Wales countryside.

Tip: **Miniature railways** are a great way to get about some of the wildlife parks listed above, including Beale Park, Cotswold Wildlife Park, Cricket St Thomas, Drusilla's Park, Knowsley Wildlife Park, Longleat and Paignton Zoo. A full-size steam train, the Jumbo Express, operates at Whipsnade.

Crossing Bridges

CARRICK A REDE
119a Whitepark Road, Ballintoy, Co. Antrim, BT54 6LS
(028 2076 9839)

One of Northern Ireland's best-loved attractions is this wobbly bridge, connecting a rocky island to the cliffs. Seven miles from Giants' Causeway, it is 40 feet long and hangs eight feet above the sea. On the island there is a children's discovery trail for eight to 14-year-olds.

CLIFTON SUSPENSION BRIDGE
Litfield Place, Clifton, Bristol, B58 (0117 974 1242)
www.clifton-suspension-bridge.org.uk

You can walk across this famous Victorian bridge, high above the Avon Gorge. Designed by the great engineer Isambard Kingdom Brunel, it was completed in 1864 in the days of horse-drawn vehicles. Today it carries a heavy volume of modern traffic: 11–12,000 vehicles a day. A visitor centre on the Leigh Woods side of the bridge is open daily 10.00am to 5.00pm. On the Clifton side, there is a Victorian 'Camera Obscura', the only one open to the public in England. Contact **Clifton Suspension Bridge Trust,** Bridgemaster's Office, Leigh Woods, Bristol BS8 3PA (0117 974 4664) for guided tours, history, heritage, talks etc.

THE LONDON BRIDGE EXPERIENCE
1-4 Tooley St, SE1 2SY (0207 403 6333) www.londonbridgeexperi-ence.com

A recently opened tour of the bridge's 2,000-year history, takes place in the vaults and excavated tombs of London Bridge itself. London Bridge has been knocked down and re-built several times, most recently in 1973 when Sir John Rennie's bridge was sold to an American oil baron, dismantled and shipped to Arizona.

THE POOHSTICKS BRIDGE
Hartfield, East Sussex

Pooh-sticks is a game invented by Winnie-the-Pooh and friends in the book *The House at Pooh Corner* by A. A. Milne. It can be played on any bridge over a river. Each person drops a stick on the upstream side of the bridge; the player whose stick first appears on the other side is the winner. A bridge in Ashdown Forest, close to the village of Hartfield, East Sussex, is thought to be the one on which A. A. Milne and his son Christopher Robin first played the game.

THE WOBBLY BRIDGE, LONDON
Millennium Bridge, Southwark, London

Cross from St Paul's Cathedral to the Tate Modern Art Gallery on the Millennium Bridge. It's a pedestrian bridge and became known as the 'wobbly bridge' because it swayed alarmingly when it was first opened. It's no longer wobbly, but the name has stuck.

London Bridge is falling down,
Falling down, falling down.
London Bridge is falling down,
My fair lady.

Seafaring and Fishy Things

HMS *BELFAST*
Morgan's Lane, Tooley Street, London, SE1 2JH (0207 940 6300)
www.hmsbelfast.iwm.org.uk
HMS *Belfast* is moored on the Thames in London. She served throughout the Second World War, playing a leading part in the destruction of the battle cruiser *Scharnhorst*, and also the Normandy Landings. In service with the Royal Navy until 1965, she was saved for the nation in 1971 as a reminder of Britain's naval past. You can go aboard and explore the ship.

BROWNSEA ISLAND
Poole, Dorset, BH13 7EE (01202 707744)
This peaceful island of woodland, wetland and heath, with a wide variety of wildlife, is famous as the birthplace of scouting and guiding. There are walks with marvellous views of Poole Harbour. Look out for red squirrels, peacocks and deer. There are special trails for young smugglers, historians and explorers. For a real adventure, travel to Brownsea Island by ferry from Poole or Sandbanks. The least expensive crossing is from Sandbanks which incidentally is the original route taken by Lord Baden Powell, founder of the scouting movement, in 1907.

THE DEEP
The Deep, Hull, HU1 4DP (01482 381000) www.thedeep.co.uk
Learn about the world's oceans and watch sharks, eels, rays and other fish in the huge 10-metre tank which holds 2.5 million litres of water

and 87 tonnes of salt. From the viewing tunnel underneath the tank, you can watch the fish as they swim above. An underwater lift takes you back to the surface.

HISTORIC DOCKYARD AT CHATHAM
Chatham, Kent, ME4 4TZ (01634 823 807)
The birthplace of many of Britain's finest sailing ships. The historic warships, including a destroyer, a submarine and a Victorian sailing sloop, can all be toured by visitors.

SS *GREAT BRITAIN*
Great Western Dockyard, Gas Ferry Road, Bristol, BS1 6TY
(0117 929 1843) www.ssgreatbritain.org
This is one of my grandchildren's favourite outings. SS *Great Britain*, designed by Isambard Kingdom Brunel, was the first ocean-going ship to have an iron hull and a screw propeller, and the largest vessel afloat when it was launched in 1843. Now she's moored in Bristol Docks and careful reconstructions give a vivid picture of the lives of passengers and crew aboard an ocean-going ship in the 19th century, including the sounds and smells.

THE *MATTHEW* OF BRISTOL
Great Western Dockyard, Gas Ferry Road, Bristol (0117-9276868)
www.matthew.co.uk
Moored near SS *Great Britain* (see above) is a modern recreation of a square-rigged sailing ship in which explorer John Cabot sailed from Bristol to North America in 1497. European explorers of that time hoped to find a sea route to Asia to trade silks and spices – but

instead of finding China or Japan, Cabot and his crew ended up in Newfoundland, Canada, and claimed it for King Henry VII. Today's *Matthew* was built by Bristol shipwrights to celebrate the 500th anniversary of that historic crossing and is now available for you to experience the extraordinary world of the Tudor sailor and explorer. Sometimes the ship leaves harbour on a voyage, or to take part in a film, so check before you go.

KIMMERIDGE BAY
Kimmeridge, Wareham, BH20 5PF (01929 481044) www. coastlink.org/kimmeridge
Kimmeridge is made for rock pooling: a rare 'double' low tide means you get four hours of uninterrupted scrabbling along the seashore. That's partly why the Purbeck Marine Wildlife Reserve is based here. Its visitor centre offers rock pool aquariums, and lots of summer events (crabbing, guided rambles, beginner's snorkel sessions).

NATIONAL MARINE AQUARIUM, PLYMOUTH
Rope Walk, Coxside, Plymouth, PL4 0LF (01752 600 301) www. national-aquarium.co.uk
With a total of 50 live exhibits, this marine aquarium displays 4,000 animals from 400 species in realistic habitats, from local shorelines to coral reefs. There are six main zones: Explorocean, The Shallows, Atlantic Reef, Mediterranean Sea, Weird Creatures and Coral Seas. (See also *Very Special Treats*, below)

NATIONAL WATERWAYS MUSEUM
Ellesmere Port, South Pier Road, Ellesmere Port, Cheshire, H65 4FW (0151 355 5017)

This is one museum divided between three locations, at Ellesmere Port, Gloucester Docks and Stoke Bruerne. It tells what it was like to live and work on our water transport system, through interactive displays, recordings of former dock and canal workers, archive film footage and other exhibits. You can climb aboard the largest collection of historic boats in the world: narrowboats, canal and river tugs, concrete barges and a steam-powered dredger.

NATIONAL WATERWAYS MUSEUM
Gloucester Docks, Llanthony Warehouse, The Docks, Gloucester, GL1 2EH (01452 318200)

AND AT: Stoke Bruerne, Nr Towcester, Northamptonshire, NN12 7SE (01604 862229)

SOUTER LIGHTHOUSE
Souter Lighthouse, Coast Road, Whitburn, Tyne & Wear SR6 7NH (01670 773966)
This was the first lighthouse in the world to use electricity. The lighthouse keeper sometimes allows children to sound the foghorn and light the light. There are stunning views over Marsden Bay and the notorious currents of 'Whitburn Steel' plus a tearoom serving local specialities, and cliff walks along The Leas where you can see nesting seasbirds on cliffs and stacks. (See the *Grace Darling Story*, on page 235)

HMS *VICTORY*
HM Naval Base, Portsmouth, Hants, PO1 3NH (023 9283 9766)
www.hms-victory.com

Nelson's flagship, best known for her role in the Battle of Trafalgar, remains a commissioned ship of the Royal Navy and the flagship of the Second Sea Lord & Commander in Chief Naval Home Command. Due to service commitments, there are occasions when she will be closed to the public for all or part of the day, so check in advance. History oozes out of the ship's timbers. The admission ticket for the ship includes entry to the Royal Naval Museum and the Trafalgar Sail. (See *Nelson at Trafalgar,* on page 250, below)

Galleries and Museums

Nowadays any Museum or Art Gallery worth its salt is child-friendly, organising quizzes and trails which make visits fun for all age groups. So if you want to give yourself a treat looking at Pre-Raphaelite paintings or French Impressionists, don't hesitate to take a grand-child along with you.

GLASGOW SCIENCE CENTRE
50 Pacific Quay, G51 1EA (0871 540 1000) www.gsc.org.uk
Children can explore four floors of hands-on exhibits, including the planetarium, climate change theatre and IMAX cinema.

IMPERIAL WAR MUSEUM
**Lambeth Road, London, SE1 6HZ (0207 416 5320)
www.iwm.org.uk**
This major exhibition is due to end on 1 January 2010. It looks at the home front in Britain through the eyes of children.

Topics such as evacuation, air raids, rationing and the blackout, are illustrated through original letters, diaries, artefacts, photographs and oral recordings. The reconstructed interior of a 1940s house shows what life was like on the home front. Perfect for projects.

THE NATIONAL GALLERY
Trafalgar Square, London, WC2N 5DN (020 7747 5923)
www.nationalgallery.org.uk
In this and other major art collections, you'll be frustrated if you try and see everything in one visit. With children, it helps to decide on a theme before you go. If you're a computerised granny, do a little homework on the gallery's website. You might decide to look at pictures with children in them, or animals, or fruit. You can hardly start too early to teach them to use their eyes, and that art is fun.

NATURAL HISTORY MUSEUM
Cromwell Road, London, SW7 5BD (020 7942 5000) www.nhm. ac.uk
Don't try and see everything, and remember to cater to your grandchildren's special interests. When we were children we went a lot, as it was quite near home. In the insect department, there were (still are, no doubt) mahogany cabinets with shallow drawers. My brother would make straight for the beetles, but I preferred the butterflies. Beware of the super-sensing T. rex. It moves and roars and my four-year-old dinosaur was absolutely terrified and had to be taken away immediately. Granny didn't feel very brave either. The museum is packed at all times. Rather than queue for food, take a picnic.

ROALD DAHL MUSEUM
81-83 High Street , Great Missenden, Bucks, HP16 OAL
(01494 892 192) www.roalddahlmuseum.org
The museum was created as a home for the author's archive in the village where he lived and wrote his books. The aim is to inspire a love of creative writing in all visitors. The Story Centre encourages everyone (young and old) to dress up, tell tales, or get arty in the craft room.

THE SCIENCE MUSEUM
Exhibition Road, South Kensington, London, SW7 2DD
(0870 870 4868) www.sciencemuseum.org.uk
The many well laid-out exhibits here will keep children entertained for hours. Mine were particularly drawn to the old-fashioned vacuum cleaners. Sadly, it never made them want to use the modern version at home.

STEPHENSON RAILWAY MUSEUM
Middle Engine Lane, North Shields, Tyne and Wear, NE29 8DX
(01912 007 145/146) www.twmuseums.org.uk/stephenson
Children can learn about the glory days of the steam railway at the Stephenson Railway Museum, and ride on a real steam train. They can see George Stephenson's Billy (c1826), a forerunner of the world-famous Rocket, and other engines from the great age of steam.

STEAM: MUSEUM OF THE GREAT WESTERN RAILWAY
Kemble Drive, Swindon, SN2 2TA (01793 466 646) www.steam-museum.org.uk
A chance to see where many of the best steam locomotives in the

world were built and to hear the stories of the men and women who worked there, not least Isambard Kingdom Brunel, the genius behind the Great Western Railway.

TATE MODERN
Bankside, London, SE1 9TG (020 7887 8888), www.tate.org.uk
A spectacular space, with something to please and intrigue children of all ages. There are free activities for children and adults to do together; the Family Zone introduces children to modern art and encourages them to think about materials, meanings and ideas; and there is always something interesting in the Turbine Hall.

VICTORIA & ALBERT MUSEUM
Cromwell Road, London, SW7 2RL (020 7942 2000) www.vam. ac.uk
The V&A always has ways of involving children. They may be able to try on a corset and crinoline, make a bookplate or build a Crystal Palace, construct a chair, have a go at tapestry weaving or try on an armour gauntlet. The new jewellery gallery is a knockout.

V&A MUSEUM OF CHILDHOOD
Cambridge Heath Road, London, E2 9PA (020 8983 5200) www. vam.ac.uk/moc
Show your grandchildren what your toys and even your great grandmother's toys looked like. There are dolls, teddy bears, toys and games dating from the 16th century onwards.

Very Special Treats

Very occasionally (perhaps once in a lifetime), you may want to treat your grandchildren, or even the whole family, to more than a great day out – something they will remember forever. Butlins, Centreparcs and Eurodisney often have discounted offers midweek, so a few days may not break the bank. And there are a number of marginally more affordable treats listed below, which still have a definite wow factor.

BUTLINS
1 Park Lane, Hemel Hempstead, Hertfordshire, HP2 4YL
(0845 070 4734) www.butlinsonline.co.uk
According to friends who swear by them, Butlins have shed their *Hi-de-hi* image and upped their game in recent years. Their three resorts at Bognor Regis, Minehead and Skegness are all situated by a good British beach. A short break offers fun for all ages, with waterworlds, sports and arts workshops and all sorts of other shows, games and activities.

CENTREPARCS
One Edison Rise, New Ollerton, Newark, Notts, NG22 9DP
(08448 267723) www.centreparcs.co.uk
Some families wax lyrical about these enclosed 'Villages'. Each is set in 400 acres of beautiful forest with lakes and streams. Choose from Whinfell Forest, Cumbria, Sherwood Forest, Nottinghamshire, Elveden Forest, Suffolk or Longleat Forest, Wiltshire. There are activities for kids of all ages to enjoy, from the Dragonflies Club, to the

Teddy Bears' Picnic, to cycling and Soccer Academy. Granny can join in, treat herself at the spa or just take it easy.

DISNEYLAND, PARIS

B.P. 100 - 77, Marne la Vallée, Ile-de-France, France (00 33 1 6030 6030) www.disneylandparis.com

An acquired taste, perhaps; some grannies may find the relentless marketing glitz a little difficult to take. The queues can be bad too. But, if you plan your trip carefully, avoiding going at peak times and are realistic about what you can get done in a few days, you will have a surprisingly good time, and your grandchildren will love you forever...

DUCK TOUR

DoSomethingDifferent.com, 3rd Floor 16 Bromells Road, London, SW4 0BG (020 8090 3790) www.dosomethingdifferent.com

Run by the company, Do Something Different, this tour of London in an amphibious vehicle is exactly that. Originally built to take troops ashore during the D-Day Landings, the DUKWs provide a novel way to see London's wonderful attractions, driving you through the streets like a minibus before sliding down a slipway into the Thames to continue the sightseeing by boat. The conspicuous yellow vehicles attract a lot of attention which, of course, the children love.

GIFFORDS CIRCUS

The Garden, Folly Farm, Bourton-on-the-Water, Glos, GL54 3BY (01451 820 378/ 0 7818 058 384) www.giffordscircus.com

There's nothing like the thrill of the big top. Gifford's Circus is a traditional English circus which tours the West Country every summer. Its tiny 'big top', which holds 360, helps to create an intimate atmosphere where the audience feels part of the show. The whole experience is sheer magic and children will want to go again and again. Highly recommended.

LEEDS CASTLE
Maidstone, Kent, ME17 1PL (01622 765400) www.leeds-castle.com
Six to 12-year-olds can become 'keeper for the day' on one of the castle's special Junior Days at the aviary. They can see what goes on behind the scenes and get involved in the daily work of a keeper, including food preparation, feeding and cleaning out. They may also help the Falconer with his Bird of Prey demonstrations, feed the swans, ducks and geese in the Duckery; lunch is part of the deal.

The Junior Keeper for the Day must be accompanied by one adult at all times. Price £50.

LEGOLAND
Windsor, Berkshire, SL4 4AY   (0871 2222001)   www.legoland. co.uk
A huge Lego theme park outside Windsor which has little to do with what you might affectionately remember as a 'quiet game of lego', but children undoubtedly love it. A one-day ticket for a child aged 3–15 costs £26 – or £23 if booked online. The price is the same for a 'senior'. Take a picnic and, in hot weather, take a towel as kids can get wet. To avoid queues for rides, arrive at opening time, go straight to the furthest away part of the park and work your way backwards.

PHILHARMONIA FAMILY DAY
Southbank Centre, Belvedere Road, London, SE1 (08716632500)
If you would like to introduce your grandchildren to classical music concerts the Philharmonia Orchestra arranges special occasional mornings to do exactly that. For five to 11-year-olds.

Spectacular Sleepovers

THE ROYAL BOTANIC GARDENS, KEW
Richmond, Surrey, TW9 3AB (020 8332 5655) www.kew.org
If your grandchildren are aged between eight and 11 take them on a Midnight Ramble: this is an all-night sleepover, involving ideally one adult – you – and four children. You will search for badgers, bats and owls, toast marshmallows around a campfire, play environmental games and sleep in 'Climbers and Creepers', Kew's botanical play zone. Costs £40 a head for both adults and children.

PLYMOUTH'S NATIONAL MARINE AQUARIUM
Rope Walk, Coxside, Plymouth, Devon, PL4 OLF (01752 600301)
www.national-aquarium.co.uk
Here, the 'shark slumber party' takes place in front of the giant shark tank and includes movies, midnight feasts and breakfast. It costs £100 for four (children must be aged five or over, and accompanied by an adult). £25 per extra person.

Car Games

I spy
One person says 'I spy with my little eye, something beginning with G...' The others ask questions until someone guesses correctly 'Grass'. Then it's his turn to spy something. Keep it simple for small children. If they don't know their letters yet, they can spy colours: 'something green'.

Red Dragon
The children look out for letter boxes. Every time they see one, they shout 'Red Dragon' and the first one to shout scores a point. First to get five points is the winner.

Finishing a word
Players take turns to say a letter, with the aim of spelling a word. The point of the game is to avoid finishing a word. For example, the players before you may say C, A, L. If all you can think of is another L, you lose the point because you complete a word: Call. But if you can think of another word, you say the next letter. It might be C. The next player can continue to spell a word starting C, A, L, C. If he thinks there is no such word, he can challenge you. 'Calculate!' you cry triumphantly, and he loses a point for a wrong challenge. It's then your turn to start the next word.

Arms and Legs (Inn Signs)
Players take it in turns to score points from the Inn signs passed on the road (not a game to play on a motorway). Legs score plus points,

but points are deducted for arms. For example, the Coach and Horses gets 8 or more points, depending on how many horses are shown on the sign, and the Dog and Duck scores 6. The King's Arms scores minus 2. People, like the Marquess of Granby, score nothing as they have 2 arms and 2 legs. On one journey we used to do regularly, there was a pub called the Sow and Litter. The player who got that one was declared the outright winner.

Granny's Cat

Also known as 'The Parson's Cat'. The first player describes Granny's Cat with an adjective beginning with A, the second with B and so on, through the alphabet. Each player has to remember the earlier adjectives. For example, 'Granny's cat is an Arrogant cat.' 'Granny's cat is an Arrogant, Beastly cat.' Towards the end it gets difficult: 'Granny's cat is an Arrogant, Beastly, Cuddly, Disgusting, Elegant, Funny, Horrible, Ill, Jealous, Kittenish, Lovely, Miaowing...'

♠5♠

Songs, Rhymes and Stories

(O)ur memories are stuffed with rhymes, poetry and stories from different stages of our lives. They float to the surface from time to time. When changing a grandchild's nappy, for example, the words of 'One two three four five / Once I caught a fish alive' came, from nowhere, into my head. I recited it, the baby laughed, and it became part of my nappy-changing routine. A selection of such rhymes appears here, in case you have forgotten them.

NURSERY RHYMES

Wee Willie Winkie runs through the town,
Upstairs and downstairs in his nightgown,
Tapping at the window and crying through the lock,
Are all the children in their beds, it's past eight o'clock?

*

There was a crooked man, who walked a crooked mile,
He found a crooked sixpence upon a crooked stile.
He bought a crooked cat which caught a crooked mouse,
And they all lived together in a little crooked house.

Diddle, diddle dumpling,
My son, John,
Went to bed
With his trousers on;
One shoe off
And one shoe on,
Diddle, diddle dumpling,
My son, John.

*

Here we go round the mulberry bush
The mulberry bush, the mulberry bush
Here we go round the mulberry bush
So early in the morning.

This is the way we wash our clothes
Wash our clothes, wash our clothes
This is the way we wash our clothes
So early Monday morning

This is the way we iron our clothes
Iron our clothes, iron our clothes
This is the way we iron our clothes
So early Tuesday morning

This is the way we mend our clothes
Mend our clothes, mend our clothes
This is the way we mend our clothes
So early Wednesday morning

This is the way we sweep the floor

Sweep the floor, sweep the floor
This is the way we sweep the floor
So early Thursday morning

This is the way we scrub the floor
Scrub the floor, scrub the floor
This is the way we scrub the floor
So early Friday morning

This is the way we bake our bread
Bake our bread, bake our bread
This is the way we bake our bread
So early Saturday morning

This is the way we go to church
Go to church, go to church
This is the way we go to church
So early Sunday morning

*

London Bridge is falling down,
Falling down,
Falling down.
London Bridge is falling down,
My fair lady.

How will we build it up again,
Up again, up again,
How will we build it up again,
My fair lady?

Build it up with silver and gold,
silver and gold, silver and gold.
Build it up with silver and gold,
My fair lady.

Gold and silver I have none,
I have none, I have none.
Gold and silver I have none,
My fair lady.

Build it up with iron and steel,
iron and steel, iron and steel.
Build it up with iron and steel,
My fair lady.

Iron and steel will bend and bow,
Bend and bow, bend and bow.
Iron and steel will bend and bow,
My fair lady.

Build it up with wood and clay,
Wood and clay, wood and clay.
Build it up with wood and clay,
My fair lady.

Wood and clay will wash away,
Wash away, wash away.
Wood and clay will wash away,
My fair lady.

Build it up with stone so strong,
Stone so strong, stone so strong.

Build it up with stone so strong,
My fair lady.

Stone so strong will last so long,
Last so long, last so long.
Stone so strong will last so long,
My fair lady.

*

Monday's child is fair of face;
Tuesday's child is full of grace;
Wednesday's child is full of woe;
Thursday's child has far to go;
Friday's child is loving and giving;
Saturday's child works hard for a living;
The child that is born on the Sabbath day,
Is bonny, and blithe, and good, and gay.

*

Solomon Grundy, born on Monday,
Christened on Tuesday, married on Wednesday,
Took ill on Thursday, worse on Friday,
Died on Saturday, buried on Sunday —
That was the end of Solomon Grundy.

*

There was an old woman tossed up in a basket
Seventeen times as high as the moon
Where was she going I could not but ask her

For in her hand she carried a broom.
'Old woman, old woman, old woman,' quoth I
'Where are you going to up so high?'
'I'm going to sweep cobwebs off the sky.'
'May I come with you?"
'Yes, bye and bye'.

*

Crosspatch, draw the latch
Sit by the fire and spin;
Take a cup and drink it up
And invite your neighbours in.

*

If all the world were treacle,
And all the sea was ink,
And all the trees were bread and cheese,
What should we have to drink?

*

Pease-pudding hot, pease-pudding cold,
Pease-pudding in the pot, nine days old.
Some like it hot, some like it cold,
Some like it in the pot, nine days old.

*

Doctor Foster went to Gloucester
All in a shower of rain,'

He stepped in a puddle
Right up to his middle
And never went there again.

*

A farmer went trotting [For bouncing small children on knee]
Upon his grey mare:
Bumpety, bumpety, bump!
With his daughter behind him
So rosy and fair;
Bumpety, bumpety, bump!

A raven cried, 'croak'
And they all tumbled down;
Bumpety, bumpety, bump!
The mare broke his knees
And the farmer his crown
Bumpety, bumpety, bump!

*

Matthew, Mark, Luke and John,
Bless the bed that I lie on.
Four corners to my bed,
Four angels round my head —
One to sing and one to pray,
And two to carry my soul away.

*

COUNTING RHYMES

One two three four five,
Once I caught a fish alive.
Six seven eight nine ten,
then I let it go again.
Why did you let it go?
Because it bit my finger so,
Which finger did it bite?
This little finger on the right.

*

One two, buckle my shoe.
Three four, knock at the door.
Five six, pick up sticks.
Seven eight, lay them straight.
Nine ten, a big fat hen.
Eleven twelve, dig and delve.
Thirteen fourteen, maids a courting.
Fifteen sixteen, maids in the kitchen.
Seventeen eighteen, maids a waiting.
Nineteen twenty, my plate's empty.

*

Ten green bottles
Hanging on the wall,
Ten green bottles
Hanging on the wall,
And if one green bottle
Should accidentally fall,

There'd be nine green bottles,
Hanging on the wall,
Nine green bottles...etc

*

One man went to mow,
Went to mow a meadow,
One man and his dog,
Went to mow a meadow
Two men went to mow,
Went to mow a meadow,
Two men, one man and his dog,
Went to mow a meadow.
Three men went to mow,
Went to mow a meadow,
Three men, two men, one man and his dog,
Went to mow a meadow.
Four men went to mow,
Went to mow a meadow,

Four men, three men, two men, one man and his dog,
Went to mow a meadow.

✳

This is the house that Jack built!
This is the malt that lay in the house that Jack built.
This is the rat that ate the malt
That lay in the house that Jack built.

This is the cat that killed the rat
That ate the malt that lay in the house that Jack built.
This is the dog that worried the cat
That killed the rat that ate the malt
That lay in the house that Jack built.

This is the cow with the crumpled horn
That tossed the dog that worried the cat
That killed the rat that ate the malt
That lay in the house that Jack built.

This is the maiden all forlorn
That milked the cow with the crumpled horn
That tossed the dog that worried the cat
That killed the rat that ate the malt
That lay in the house that Jack built.

This is the man all tattered and torn
That kissed the maiden all forlorn
That milked the cow with the crumpled horn
That tossed the dog that worried the cat
That killed the rat that ate the malt

That lay in the house that Jack built.

This is the priest all shaven and shorn
That married the man all tattered and torn
That kissed the maiden all forlorn
That milked the cow with the crumpled horn
That tossed the dog that worried the cat
That killed the rat that ate the malt
That lay in the house that Jack built.

This is the cock that crowed in the morn
That waked the priest all shaven and shorn
That married the man all tattered and torn
That kissed the maiden all forlorn
That milked the cow with the crumpled horn
That tossed the dog that worried the cat
That killed the rat that ate the malt
That lay in the house that Jack built.

This is the farmer sowing his corn
That kept the cock that crowed in the morn
That waked the priest all shaven and shorn
That married the man all tattered and torn
That kissed the maiden all forlorn
That milked the cow with the crumpled horn
That tossed the dog that worried the cat
That killed the rat that ate the malt
That lay in the house that Jack built!

*

On the first day of Christmas

my true love sent to me
A partridge in a pear tree.

On the second day of Christmas,
my true love sent to me
Two turtle doves,
And a partridge in a pear tree.

On the third day of Christmas,
my true love sent to me
Three French hens,
Two turtle doves,
And a partridge in a pear tree.

On the fourth day of Christmas,
my true love sent to me
Four calling birds,
Three French hens,
Two turtle doves,
And a partridge in a pear tree.

On the fifth day of Christmas,
my true love sent to me
Five gold rings,
Four calling birds,
Three French hens,
Two turtle doves,
And a partridge in a pear tree.

On the sixth day of Christmas,
my true love sent to me

Six geese a-laying,
Five gold rings,
Four calling birds,
Three French hens,
Two turtle doves,
And a partridge in a pear tree.

On the seventh day of Christmas,
my true love sent to me
Seven swans a-swimming,
Six geese a-laying,
Five gold rings,
Four calling birds,
Three French hens,
Two turtle doves,
And a partridge in a pear tree.

On the eighth day of Christmas,
my true love sent to me
Eight maids a-milking,
Seven swans a-swimming,
Six geese a-laying,
Five gold rings,
Four calling birds,
Three French hens,
Two turtle doves,
And a partridge in a pear tree.

On the ninth day of Christmas,
my true love sent to me
Nine ladies dancing,
Eight maids a-milking,

Seven swans a-swimming,
Six geese a-laying,
Five gold rings,
Four calling birds,
Three French hens,
Two turtle doves,
And a partridge in a pear tree.

On the tenth day of Christmas,
my true love sent to me
Ten lords a-leaping,
Nine ladies dancing,
Eight maids a-milking,
Seven swans a-swimming,
Six geese a-laying,
Five gold rings,
Four calling birds,
Three French hens,
Two turtle doves,
And a partridge in a pear tree.

On the eleventh day of Christmas,
my true love sent to me
Eleven pipers piping,
Ten lords a-leaping,
Nine ladies dancing,
Eight maids a-milking,
Seven swans a-swimming,
Six geese a-laying,
Five gold rings,
Four calling birds,
Three French hens,

Two turtle doves,
And a partridge in a pear tree.

On the twelfth day of Christmas,
my true love sent to me
Twelve drummers drumming,
Eleven pipers piping,
Ten lords a-leaping,
Nine ladies dancing,
Eight maids a-milking,
Seven swans a-swimming,
Six geese a-laying,
Five gold rings,
Four calling birds,
Three French hens,
Two turtle doves,
And a partridge in a pear tree!

CAMPFIRE SONGS

On top of spaghetti all covered with cheese,
I lost my poor meatball when somebody sneezed.

It rolled off the table, it rolled on to the floor,
And then my poor meatball rolled out of the door.

It rolled into the garden and under a bush,
And then my poor meatball was nothing but mush.

The mush was as tasty as tasty could be,
And early next summer it grew to a tree.

The tree was all covered with beautiful moss.
It grew great big meatballs and tomato sauce.

So if you eat spaghetti all covered with cheese,
Hold on to your meatball and don't ever sneeze.

*

The bear went over the mountain,
The bear went over the mountain,
To see what he could see
To see what he could see,
To see what he could see.
The other side of the mountain,
The other side of the mountain,
The other side of the mountain,
Was all that he could see.

Was all that he could see,
Was all that he could see,
The other side of the mountain,
Was all that he could see!

*

There's a hole in my bucket, (round)
Dear Liza, dear Liza
There's a hole in my bucket,
Dear Liza, a hole.

Then fix it, dear Henry,
Dear Henry, dear Henry
Then fix it, dear Henry,
Dear Henry, fix it.

With what shall I fix it,
Dear Liza, dear Liza?
With what shall I fix it,
Dear Liza, with what?

With a straw, dear Henry,
Dear Henry, dear Henry
With a straw, dear Henry,
Dear Henry, with a straw.

But the straw is too long,
Dear Liza, dear Liza
But the straw is too long,
Dear Liza, too long

Then cut it, dear Henry,
Dear Henry, dear Henry
Then cut it, dear Henry,
Dear Henry, cut it.

With what shall I cut it,
Dear Liza, dear Liza?
With what shall I cut it,
Dear Liza, with what?

With an axe, dear Henry,
Dear Henry, dear Henry

With an axe, dear Henry,
Dear Henry, an axe.

The axe is too dull,
Dear Liza, dear Liza
The axe is too dull,
Dear Liza, too dull

Then sharpen it, dear Henry,
Dear Henry, dear Henry
Then sharpen it, dear Henry,
Dear Henry, sharpen it.

With what shall I sharpen it,
Dear Liza, dear Liza?
With what shall I sharpen it,
Dear Liza, with what?

With a stone, dear Henry,
Dear Henry, dear Henry
With a stone, dear Henry,
Dear Henry, a stone.

The stone is too dry,
Dear Liza, dear Liza
The stone is too dry,
Dear Liza, too dry

Then wet it, dear Henry,
Dear Henry, dear Henry
Then wet it, dear Henry,
Dear Henry, wet it.

With what shall I wet it,
Dear Liza, dear Liza?
With what shall I wet it,
Dear Liza, with what?

With water, dear Henry,
Dear Henry, dear Henry
With water, dear Henry,
Dear Henry, with water.

How shall I get it,
Dear Liza, dear Liza,
How shall I get it,
Dear Liza, how shall I?

In the bucket, dear Henry,
Dear Henry, dear Henry
In the bucket, dear Henry,
Dear Henry, in the bucket.

There's a hole in the bucket, etc

NONSENSE RHYMES AND POEMS

Caesar ad sum jam forte
Pompey aderat,
Caesar sic in omnibus
Pompey sic in at

There was an old man named Michael Finnegan
He had whiskers on his chinnegan
They fell out and then grew in again
Poor old Michael Finnegan
Begin again.

There was an old man named Michael Finnegan
He went fishing with a pinnegan
Caught a fish and dropped it in again
Poor old Michael Finnegan
Begin again.

There was an old man named Michael Finnegan
He grew fat and then grew thin again
Then he died and had to begin again
Poor old Michael Finnegan
Begin again.

✳

One fine day, in the middle of the night
Two dead men got up to fight
Back to back they fought each other
Drew their swords and shot each other

✳

No more Latin, no more French
No more sitting on the hard school bench
When the teacher
Rings the bell
All our books may go to hell

There was an old woman who swallowed a fly
I don't know why she swallowed a fly,
Perhaps she'll die.

There was an old woman who swallowed a spider,
That wriggled and jiggled and tickled inside her,
She swallowed the spider to catch the fly,
I don't know why she swallowed the fly,
Perhaps she'll die.

There was an old woman who swallowed a bird,
How absurd! to swallow a bird,
She swallowed the bird to catch the spider,
That wriggled and jiggled and tickled inside her,
She swallowed the spider to catch the fly,
I don't know why she swallowed the fly,
Perhaps she'll die.

There was an old woman who swallowed a cat,
Imagine that! to swallow a cat,
She swallowed the cat to catch the bird,
She swallowed the bird to catch the spider,
That wriggled and jiggled and tickled inside her,
She swallowed the spider to catch the fly,
I don't know why she swallowed the fly,
Perhaps she'll die.

There was an old woman who swallowed a dog,
What a hog! to swallow a dog,
She swallowed the dog to catch the cat,
She swallowed the cat to catch the bird,
She swallowed the bird to catch the spider,

That wriggled and jiggled and tickled inside her,
She swallowed the spider to catch the fly,
I don't know why she swallowed the fly,
Perhaps she'll die.

There was an old woman who swallowed a goat,
Just opened her throat! to swallow a goat,
She swallowed the goat to catch the dog,
She swallowed the dog to catch the cat,
She swallowed the cat to catch the bird,
She swallowed the bird to catch the spider,
That wriggled and jiggled and tickled inside her,
She swallowed the spider to catch the fly,
I don't know why she swallowed the fly,
Perhaps she'll die.

There was an old woman who swallowed a cow,
I don't know how she swallowed a cow!
She swallowed the cow to catch the goat,
She swallowed the goat to catch the dog,
She swallowed the dog to catch the cat,
She swallowed the cat to catch the bird,
She swallowed the bird to catch the spider,
That wriggled and jiggled and tickled inside her,
She swallowed the spider to catch the fly,
I don't know why she swallowed the fly,
Perhaps she'll die.

There was an old woman who swallowed a horse,
She's dead — of course!

The Abominable Snowman
[By Ogden Nash]
I've never seen an abominable snowman,
I'm hoping not to see one,
I'm also hoping, if I do,
That it will be a wee one.

*

Custard the Dragon
[By Ogden Nash]
Custard the dragon had big sharp teeth,
And spikes on top of him and scales underneath,
Mouth like a fireplace, chimney for a nose,
And realio, trulio, daggers on his toes.

*

The Octopus [By Ogden Nash]
Tell me, O Octopus, I begs
Is those things arms, or is they legs?
I marvel at thee, Octopus;
If I were thou, I'd call me Us.

*

Algy met a bear
And the bear met Algy.
The bear was bulgy
And the bulge was Algy.

A sailor went to sea, sea, sea
To see what he could see, see, see
But all that he could see, see, see
Was the bottom of the deep blue sea, sea, sea.

✳

The Hippopotamus Song
[Flanders and Swann — to be sung in part]
A bold hippopotamus was standing one day
On the banks of the cool Shalimar.
He gazed at the bottom as he peacefully lay
By the light of the evening star.
Away on the hilltop sat combing her hair
His fair hippopotami maid.
The hippopotamus was no ignoramus
And sang her this sweet serenade:

Chorus:
Mud, mud, glorious mud,
Nothing quite like it for cooling the blood,
So follow me follow, down to the hollow
And there let us wallow in glorious mud.

✳

There was a cow from Huddersfield,
She was a cow that wouldn't yield,
The reason why she wouldn't yield?
She didn't like her udders feeled.

The common cormorant or shag
[By Christopher Isherwood]
Lays eggs inside a paper bag
The reason you will see no doubt
It is to keep the lightning out
But what these unobservant birds
Have never noticed is that herds
Of wandering bears may come with buns
And steal the bags to hold the crumbs.

*

Colonel Fazackerley Butterworth-Toast [by Charles Causley]
Bought an old castle complete with a ghost,
But someone or other forgot to declare
To Colonel Fazak that the spectre was there.

On the very first evening, while waiting to dine,
The Colonel was taking a fine sherry wine,
When the ghost, with a furious flash and a flare,
Shot out of the chimney and shivered, 'Beware!'

Colonel Fazackerley put down his glass
And said, 'My dear fellow, that's really first class!
I just can't conceive how you do it at all.
I imagine you're going to a Fancy Dress Ball?'

At this, the dread ghost made a withering cry.
Said the Colonel (his monocle firm in his eye),
'Now just how you do it, I wish I could think.
Do sit down and tell me, and please have a drink.'

The ghost in his phosphorous cloak gave a roar
And floated about between ceiling and floor.
He walked through a wall and returned through a pane
And backed up the chimney and came down again.

Said the Colonel, 'With laughter I'm feeling quite weak!'
(As trickles of merriment ran down his cheek).
'My house-warming party I hope you won't spurn.
You MUST say you'll come and you'll give us a turn!'

At this, the poor spectre - quite out of his wits —
Proceeded to shake himself almost to bits.
He rattled his chains and he clattered his bones
And he filled the whole castle with mumbles and moans.

But Colonel Fazackerley, just as before,
Was simply delighted and called out, 'Encore!'
At which the ghost vanished, his efforts in vain,
And never was seen at the castle again.

'Oh dear, what a pity!' said Colonel Fazak.
'I don't know his name, so I can't call him back.'
And then with a smile that was hard to define,
Colonel Fazackerley went in to dine.

*

Winkin', Blinkin', and Nod,
one night sailed off in a wooden shoe;
Sailed off on a river of crystal light into a sea of dew.
'Where are you going and what do you wish?' the old moon asked the three.
'We've come to fish for the herring fish that live in this beautiful sea.

Nets of silver and gold have we,' said Winkin', Blinkin', and Nod.
The old moon laughed and sang a song as they rocked in the wooden shoe.
And the wind that sped them all night long ruffled the waves of dew.
Now the little stars are the herring fish that live in that beautiful sea;
'Cast your nets wherever you wish, never afraid are we!'
So cried the stars to the fishermen three — Winkin', and Blinkin', and Nod.
So all night long their nets they threw to the stars in the twinkling foam.
'Til down from the skies came the wooden shoe bringing the fishermen home.

*

From **The Hunting of the Snark** [by Lewis Carroll]
There was one who was famed for the number of things
He forgot when he entered the ship:
His umbrella, his watch, all his jewels and rings,
And the clothes he had bought for the trip.

He had forty-two boxes, all carefully packed,
With his name painted clearly on each:
But, since he omitted to mention the fact,
They were all left behind on the beach.

The loss of his clothes hardly mattered, because
He had seven coats on when he came,
With three pairs of boots—but the worst of it was,
He had wholly forgotten his name.

He would answer to 'Hi!' or to any loud cry,
Such as 'Fry me!' or 'Fritter my wig!'
To 'What-you-may-call-um!' or 'What-was-his-name!'
But especially 'Thing-um-a-jig!'

From **You are old, Father William** [by Lewis Carroll]
'You are old, Father William,' the young man said,
'And your hair has become very white;
And yet you incessantly stand on your head
Do you think, at your age, it is right?'

'In my youth,' Father William replied to his son,
'I feared it might injure the brain;
But, now that I'm perfectly sure I have none,
Why, I do it again and again.'

'You are old,' said the youth, 'as I mentioned before,
And have grown most uncommonly fat;
Yet you turned a back-somersault in at the door —
Pray, what is the reason of that?'

'In my youth,' said the sage, as he shook his grey locks,
'I kept all my limbs very supple
By the use of this ointment — one shilling the box —
Allow me to sell you a couple?'

*

Silly Old Baboon [by Spike Milligan]
There was a baboon
Who one afternoon
Said I think I will fly to the sun
So with two great palms
strapped to his arms
he started his takeoff run

Mile after mile

He galloped in style
But never once left the ground
You're going too slow said a passing crow
Try reaching the speed of sound

SO
He put on a spurt
My God how it hurt
Both the soles of his feet caught on fire
As he went through a stream
There were great clouds of steam
But he never got any higher

On and on through the night
Both his knees caught alight
Clouds of smoke billowed out of his rear!
Quick to his aid
Were the fire brigade
They chased him for over a year

Many moons passed by
Did Baboon ever fly
Did he ever get to the sun?
I've just heard today,
He's well on his way
He'll be passing through Acton at one.

PS — well, what do you expect from a baboon.

*

Jabberwocky [by Lewis Carroll]
'Twas brillig, and the slithy toves
Did gyre and gimble in the wabe:
All mimsy were the borogoves,
And the mome raths outgrabe.
'Beware the Jabberwock, my son!
The jaws that bite, the claws that catch!
Beware the Jubjub bird, and shun
The frumious Bandersnatch!'
He took his vorpal sword in hand:
Long time the manxome foe he sought —
So rested he by the Tumtum tree,
And stood awhile in thought.
And, as in uffish thought he stood,
The Jabberwock, with eyes of flame,
Came whiffling through the tulgey wood,
And burbled as it came!
One, two! One, two! And through and through
The vorpal blade went snicker-snack!
He left it dead, and with its head
He went galumphing back.
'And, has thou slain the Jabberwock?
Come to my arms, my beamish boy!
O frabjous day! Callooh! Callay!'
He chortled in his joy.

'Twas brillig, and the slithy toves
Did gyre and gimble in the wabe;
All mimsy were the borogoves,
And the mome raths outgrabe.

*

The Great Panjandrum [By Samuel Foote]
So she went into the garden
to cut a cabbage-leaf
to make an apple-pie;
and at the same time
a great she-bear, coming down the street,
pops its head into the shop.
What! no soap?
So he died,
and she very imprudently married the Barber:
and there were present
the Picninnies,
and the Joblillies,
and the Garyulies,
and the great Panjandrum himself,
with the little round button at top;
and they all fell to playing the game of catch-as-catch-can,
till the gunpowder ran out at the heels of their boots.

PARODIES

While shepherds washed their socks by night
All seated round the tub
A bar of Sunlight soap came down
And they began to rub

✳

We Three Kings of Orient are
One on a bicycle, one in a car

One on a scooter, tooting his hooter
Which didn't get very far

*

Oh dear what can the matter be
Three old ladies got locked in the lavatory
They were there from Monday to Saturday
Nobody knew they were there

*

Good King Wenceslas looked out
On his cabbage garden
Bumped into a brussels sprout
And said I beg your pardon

Sliding down the banisters
Eating raw bananas
Where d'you think he put the skin?
Down the Queen's pyjamas

*

Hey diddle, diddle
The cat did a piddle
Behind the kitchen door
The little dog laughed to see such fun
so the cat did a little bit more.

*

Row, row, row your boat
Gently down the stream
Throw your teacher overboard
And listen to her scream

*

Twinkle, twinkle, little bat!
How I wonder what you're at!
Up above the world you fly,
Like a tea-tray in the sky.

*

Mary had a little lamb
She kept it on a shelf
And every time it wagged its tail
It spanked its little self

*

Ladles and Jellyspoons
Take my advice
Take off your knickers
And slide on the ice

*

Adam and Eve and Pinch Me
Went down to the river to bathe
Adam and Eve were drowned
And who do you think was saved?

Pinch punch the first of the month
and no returns or 'rabbits and hares'

& TWO PALINDROMES:

Able was I ere I saw Elba

Madam I'm Adam

TONGUE TWISTERS

Red leather yellow leather
Red leather yellow leather

*

Peter piper picked a peck of pickled pepper
If Peter piper picked a peck of pickled pepper
How many pecks of pickled pepper
Did Peter piper pick?

*

Sister Susie sewing shirts for soldiers
Such saucy soft shirts Sister Susie sews
Some soldiers write epistles
Saying they'd rather sleep on thistles
Then wear the saucy soft shirts
That Sister Susie sews

How much wood would a woodchuck chuck
If a woodchuck could chuck wood?
A woodchuck would chuck as much as a woodchuck could chuck
If a woodchuck could chuck wood.

✳

Betty Botter bought some butter
But she said the butter's bitter,
If I put it in my batter
It will make my batter bitter,
But a bit of better butter
Will make my batter better,
So she bought some better butter
Better than the bitter butter,
And she put it in her batter
And her batter was not bitter,
So 'twas better Betty Botter
Bought a bit of better butter.

✳

Two toads, totally tired, tried to trot to Tetbury

✳

She sells seashells on the sea shore
The shells that she sells are seashells, I'm sure.
So if she sells shells on the seashore,
I'm sure that the shells are seashore shells.

TALES TO TELL

The Boy who Saved Holland

Holland is a country where much of the land lies below sea level. Only the dikes keep the North Sea from flooding the land. For centuries the people of Holland have worked to keep the walls, or dikes, strong so that their country will be safe and dry. Even a hole no larger than your finger can be very dangerous.

Many years ago there lived in Holland a boy named Peter. Peter's father was one of the men who tended the gates in the dikes, called sluices. He opened and closed the sluices so that ships could pass out of Holland's canals into the sea.

When Peter was eight, his mother called him one afternoon, 'I want you to go across the dike and take these cakes to your friend, the blind boy. If you go quickly, and do not stop to play, you will be home again before dark.' Peter visited his friend and talked to him about his walk along the dike and the ships far out at sea. Then he said goodbye and set out for home.

As he walked beside the canal, he noticed how the rains had swollen the waters, and how they beat against the side of the dike, and he thought of his father's gates. 'I'm glad they are strong,' he said to himself. 'If they gave way that what would be become of us?' Suddenly he noticed that the sun was setting. 'Mother will be watching for me,' he thought, and he began to run towards home.

Just then he heard a noise. It was the sound of trickling water! He stopped and looked down. There was a small hole in the dike. Peter understood the danger at once. If the water ran through a little hole it would soon make a larger one, and the whole country would be flooded. In a moment he saw what he must do. Quickly he scrambled down the side of the dike and pushed his finger into the tiny hole. The flow of water stopped!

'I must keep the water back with my finger,' he said to himself. 'Holland shall not drown while I am here.' This was all very well at first, but it soon grew dark and cold. Peter shouted for someone to come and help him. But nobody heard him. It grew colder, and his arm ached, and began to grow stiff and numb. He shouted again. But still no one came. His mother had looked for him along the dike road many times, and now she had closed and locked the cottage door, thinking that Peter must be spending the night with his blind friend.

Peter tried to whistle, but his teeth chattered with the cold. He thought of his family in their warm beds. 'I must not let them be drowned,' he thought. 'I must stay here until someone comes, even if I have to stay all night.' The moon and stars looked down on the child crouching on the side of the dike. His head was bent, and his eyes were closed, but he was not asleep. He stayed there all night keeping the angry waters out.

Early next morning, a man going to work heard a groan as he walked along the top of the dike. Looking over the edge, he saw a child clinging to the side of the dike. 'What's the matter?' he called. 'Are you hurt?' 'I'm keeping the angry waters back!' Peter called. 'Tell them to come quickly!'

The alarm was spread. People came running with shovels and the hole was soon mended. They carried Peter home to his parents, and before long the whole town knew how he had saved their lives that night. To this day, they have never forgotten the brave little hero of Holland. There is a statue of Peter in the small town of Spaarndam.

*

Grace Darling, the Lighthouse Keeper's Daughter

GRACE DARLING WAS BORN nearly two hundred years ago in Northumberland. From the age of ten she lived with her family in a lighthouse at Longstone in the Farne Islands, where her father was the lighthouse keeper.

The lighthouse was built on bare rock, only a metre above the waves at high tide. It was bleak, and lonely, exposed to the full fury of the North Sea.

Grace's father worked hard. Every day he polished the brass reflectors and cleaned the lamps and the windows of the lighthouse lantern. In those days lighthouses were run on oil and not electricity and so he had to check the wicks and make sure there was enough oil in the lamps. He also kept records of the tides and made sure the lighthouse was kept in good repair. Grace also took her turn at the top of the lighthouse, keeping watch, day and night, for ships in trouble at sea and sometimes she helped her father when he went out in the boat.

On 5 September 1838, when Grace was 22, the steamship *Forfarshire* set off from Hull to Dundee in Scotland, carrying a cargo of cloth, hardware and soap, and about 60 passengers and crew. Next day the ship's boiler began to leak, then the engine stopped. With no power to drive her, the *Forfarshire* began to drift. Suddenly, at around four in the morning, there was a great crash as the steamship struck the Big Harcar rock. There was no time to call the passengers from their cabins and get them into the lifeboats. Within fifteen minutes the ship had broken in two. The back half was swept away and sank with over 48 people on board.

On that terrible night, only Grace and her parents were in the lighthouse. A fierce storm blew and huge waves battered the lighthouse walls. It was Grace who spotted the wreck shortly after it hit the rock, but it was not until nearly seven o'clock in the morning that it was light enough to see survivors moving on Big Harcar Rock. William Darling, her father, realised that the appalling conditions would prevent the launching of the North Sunderland lifeboat. He would have to go himself. The only person who could help him was Grace.

Grace took blankets to warm the survivors and father and daughter set off. The tide and wind were so strong that they had to row for almost a mile to avoid the jagged rocks and reach the survivors safely.

There were nine people still alive on the rock but their rowing boat could only take five in the first rescue trip. William leapt out of the boat and on to the rock, leaving Grace to handle the boat alone. To keep it in one place, she had to take both oars and row backwards and forwards, trying to keep the boat from being smashed against the reef. On the rock, William found eight men, including one who was badly injured. There was also a woman, holding her two children, who were both dead. Grace's father and three of the men rowed the boat back to the lighthouse, taking with them Grace, the injured man and woman. Grace then remained at the lighthouse and looked after the survivors with her mother. Her father and two of the *Forfarshire* crew returned for the other four men.

The story of the wreck and the daring rescue made the front pages of all the newspapers. Grace Darling became a heroine. Everyone wanted to know what she looked like. Since there were no televisions or cameras in those days, many artists came to the lighthouse to paint Grace's portrait instead.

Both Grace and her father were awarded gold medals from the Royal Humane Society and Silver Medals from the National

Institution for the Preservation of Life from Shipwreck (now the RNLI) and Queen Victoria sent Grace £50.

There is a monument to her in St Aidan's churchyard in Bamburgh. Today, nearly 170 years later, a lifeboat named *Grace Darling* operates at Seahouses lifeboat station.

*

William Tell

ABOUT SEVEN HUNDRED YEARS ago Switzerland was governed by a man called Hermann Gessler. He was in the service of the Austrian Emperor, and his harsh ways had made him very unpopular.

One day William Tell walked into a village named Altdorf, with his little son. He came from the nearby hamlet of Bürglen, and was thought to be the best crossbowman and the best handler of a boat in the region. He either ignored or did not see a hat set atop a long pole that stood in the marketplace. Some soldiers approached him, and asked him how he dared walk past the Governor's hat without bowing down.

Then Governor Gessler himself arrived and the soldiers told him that William Tell would not bow to the hat.

'I have heard of your skill with the crossbow,' said the cruel Governor to William Tell. 'Now, let us see if the tales are true. Take that boy and tie him to that linden tree.'

William Tell watched in horror as his son was dragged from him, and bound to the trunk of the tree.

'Now set this apple on his head,' said Gessler. 'And if you can split that apple with your arrow I will spare your life.'

'I cannot do that, your grace,' said Tell. 'What if I miss? I cannot aim at my own child.'

'Then he shall be killed in your sight,' said Gessler. 'Come, I wish to see a display of your skill.'

Reluctantly Tell drew two arrows from his quiver, and set one in his belt. The second he fitted to his bow, and set it upon his shoulder. A moment later a loud cheer arose among the bystanders; the apple had been pierced through the centre, and fell in two equal pieces.

'A mighty shot!' said Gessler. 'But tell me – why did you take two arrows?'

'If the first arrow had hurt my child I would have killed you with the second,' said Tell.

The Governor was so angry he had William Tell seized and taken by boat to a prison across the lake.

But as they were crossing the lake, a fearful storm arose and the Governor and his men began to lose hope of ever reaching the opposite shore alive.

'Your honour,' said one of the soldiers. 'William Tell is the best helmsman in Switzerland. Let him take control of the boat – otherwise we will all be drowned!'

William Tell agreed to guide them to safety, and, taking the rudder, directed the vessel towards a large, overhanging rock. Suddenly he made a spring upwards, and, catching hold of the rock, pulled himself up and disappeared.

'Cast anchor, cast anchor!' cried Gessler. 'We cannot let him escape!'

The Governor and his men jumped ashore and set off in pursuit.

'I shall destroy Tell,' thought Gessler. 'I will kill him, and his wife, and his children…'

Before he could go any further an arrow cut through the air and entered his heart. William Tell had shot his second arrow and Gessler was dead.

Wilhelm Tell had freed the people of Switzerland from their oppressor, and they hailed him as a hero. Some even wanted to make him king, but he refused, and returned to his peaceful cottage in the mountains.

[adapted from the story as told by Bethan Lewis for Real History: see **www.jamboree.freedom-in-education.co.uk/real_history** *for all sorts of great tales.]*

✳

David and Goliath

THE PHILISTINE ARMY had gathered for war against Israel. The two armies faced each other, camped for battle on opposite sides of a steep valley. A Philistine giant, measuring over nine feet tall and wearing full armour, came out twice a day for forty days, mocking and challenging the Israelites to fight. His name was Goliath. He wanted the Israelites to send out one soldier to fight him in single combat, to decide the outcome of the battle. Saul, who was King of Israel, was terrified of Goliath, and so was his army – nobody dared to fight him.

One day David, the youngest son of Jesse, and a shepherd boy, was sent to the battle lines by his father to take food and bring back news of his brothers. David heard Goliath shouting his daily defiance and saw how he terrified the Israelites. David shouted back at Goliath, asking him defiantly how he dared to be so aggressive towards the Israelites.

Eventually David volunteered to fight Goliath, but it was difficult to persuade King Saul to let a young shepherd go out to fight the giant. It must have seemed an impossible task to defeat so strong and fierce a man.

Saul offered David his armour, but David refused. Dressed in his simple tunic, carrying his shepherd's staff, a sling (a kind of catapult) and a pouch of five stones, which he had picked out of a stream, David approached Goliath. The giant cursed him, hurling threats and insults.

David, called out to Goliath, 'You come against me with sword and spear and javelin, but I come against you in the name of the Lord Almighty, the God of the armies of Israel, whom you have defied.'

As Goliath moved in for the kill, David reached into his bag and slung one of his stones at Goliath's head. Finding a hole in the armor, the stone sank into the giant's forehead and he fell face down on the ground.

David then took Goliath's sword, killed him and cut off his head. When the Philistines saw that their hero was dead, they turned and ran. So the Israelites pursued, chasing and killing them and plundering their camp.

Battles are not always won by the mightiest and most terrifying, and the smallest and weakest don't always lose.

Robert the Bruce and the Spider

(O)n a lonely island, off the Irish coast, stood a mean and miserable hut. Inside, a man, his cloak wrapped close about him, in an attempt to keep out the freezing cold, lay on a straw pallet. A fire smoked in the centre of the rough earthen floor, and the remains of a frugal meal lay on a small wooden table.

The man was Robert Bruce, king of Scotland, who had been driven out of his own country by the king of England, Edward I. Robert Bruce's castle had been captured, his wife, the Queen, taken prisoner and he was on the run.

Robert was in despair. He wondered whether the freedom of Scotland was worth the great price that he was paying. Was it worth the lives of all those slain in battle, worth the grief of their wives and orphaned children? Perhaps, he thought, he should give up his fight for freedom and go instead to the Holy Land, to fight against the enemies of Christendom. Perhaps that would make up for the deaths that his ambitions had brought about. But how could he abandon Scotland, while there was still a chance, however slender, of success?

The wind howled; the fire had died down. Robert lay still and silent on his mean straw bed, oblivious of the cold and discomfort of his surroundings, troubled by his thoughts. Suddenly he noticed a spider hanging by a long silvery thread from one of the wooden beams above his head, and trying to swing itself to another beam. The spider tried again and again, failing every time. Six times, counted Robert, the spider tried and failed. 'Six times,' thought Robert 'I have fought against the English and failed.'

He watched the spider intently. 'If this spider fails again on the seventh attempt, I too shall give up my fight for Scotland. But if it succeeds, I shall try again.' The spider, as though aware of Robert's thought, swung itself again with all its tiny strength – and finally, on

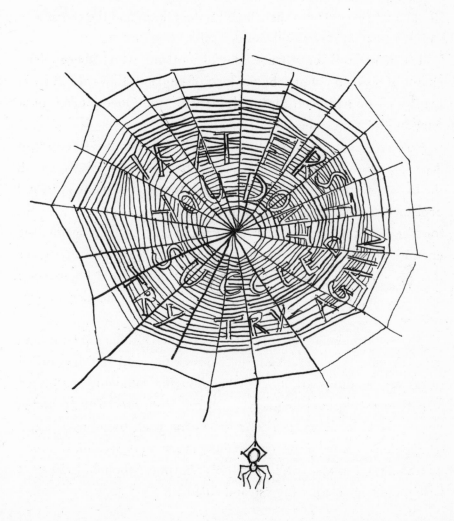

the seventh attempt, it succeeded. It swung on to the beam it had been trying to reach, and fastened its thread.

Robert Bruce smiled, and sat up. He threw off his despair and grief, and determined to set out for Scotland once more and continue his fight against the English. The fight continued for the next eight years, until 1314, when the English were defeated at the Battle of Bannockburn and finally driven out of Scotland.

If at first you don't succeed...

[*adapted from Rohini Chowdhury's history tales: see* **www.longlongtimeago. com**]

*

Casabianca, or the Boy Who Stood on the Burning Deck

IN 1798, DURING THE Battle of the Nile between the French and the English, Louis de Casabianca, the Commander of a French ship *L'Oriente* had taken his young son to sea with him. The boy, Giocante Casabianca, was 12 or 13, the age that many boys went to sea as cabin boys at that time. The French were losing the battle and *L'Oriente* was coming under cannon fire from all sides.

Before the battle began, Giocante had been given strict orders by his father to stay on deck and not to move, while his father went around the ship to see to his men. The battle began, and the boy, extremely frightened but not daring to disobey, waited on deck for his father to return. The battle was getting fiercer and already parts of the ship were on fire, but he trusted his father and so, in spite of his terror, he waited, obediently. What he didn't know was that his father had been killed by a cannon ball, which had hit the ship below deck. So he waited and waited, in the middle of the terrible noise and tumult, for a father who would never return.

The ship was by then well and truly on fire and the crew of the *L'Oriente* had forgotten all about the little cabin boy in their fear and haste to escape. They knew that there was a stock of gunpowder on board which would explode and blow the ship to pieces when the fire reached it. But young Casabianca refused to desert his post without orders from his father and so perished when the flames caused the magazine to explode.

His death inspired a poem 'Casabianca' which is said to have remained one of the most popular poems ever written:

*

'Casabianca'
by Felicia Hemans (1793-1835)

The boy stood on the burning deck
Whence all but he had fled;
The flame that lit the battle's wreck
Shone round him o'er the dead.

Yet beautiful and bright he stood,
As born to rule the storm;
A creature of heroic blood,
A proud, though child-like form.

The flames rolled on — he would not go
Without his Father's word;
That father, faint in death below,
His voice no longer heard.

He called aloud — 'say, Father, say
If yet my task is done?'
He knew not that the chieftain lay
Unconscious of his son.

'Speak, father!' once again he cried,
'If I may yet be gone!'
And but the booming shots replied,
And fast the flames rolled on.

Upon his brow he felt their breath,
And in his waving hair,
And looked from that lone post of death
In still yet brave despair.

And shouted but once more aloud,
'My father! Must I stay?'
While o'er him fast, through sail and shroud,
The wreathing fires made way.

They wrapt the ship in splendour wild,
They caught the flag on high,
And streamed above the gallant child,
Like banners in the sky.

There came a burst of thunder sound —
The boy — oh! Where was he?

Ask of the winds that far around
With fragments strewed the sea! —

With mast, and helm, and pennon fair,
That well had borne their part—
But the noblest thing which perished there
Was that young faithful heart.

*

Dick Whittington

A LONG TIME AGO there lived a poor boy called Dick Whittington. He had no mother and no father, and often nothing to eat. One day he heard of the great city of London, where, said everyone, the streets were paved with gold. Dick decided to go to London to seek his fortune.

London was a big and busy city and Dick could not find any streets that were paved with gold. Tired, cold and hungry he fell asleep on the steps of a great house. It belonged to Mr Fitzwarren, a rich merchant who was a good and generous man. He took Dick into his house, and gave him work as a scullery boy.

Dick had a little room of his own where he could have been very happy if it had not been for the rats. They would run all over him as he lay on his bed at night and would not let him sleep. One day Dick earned a penny shining shoes for a gentleman, and with it he bought a cat.

After that Dick's life became easier — the cat frightened away the rats, and Dick could sleep in peace at night.

One day Mr Fitzwarren called all the servants of the house together. One of his ships was leaving for a far-off land with goods to trade.

Mr Fitzwarren asked his servants to send something of their own in the ship if they so desired, something which could perhaps be traded for a bit of gold or money. Dick had only his cat to send – which he did with a sad heart.

Dick continued to work as a scullery boy for Mr Fitzwarren, who was very kind to him. But there was a cook who made Dick's life so miserable that finally Dick decided to run away. He had almost reached the end of the city when he heard Bow Bells ring out. 'Turn again Whittington, thrice Lord Mayor of London', chimed the bells. Dick was astonished – but he did as the bells said and went back to Mr Fitzwarren.

When he returned he found that Mr Fitzwarren's ship had returned, and that his cat had been sold for a great fortune to the King of Barbary whose palace had been overrun with mice. Dick had become a rich man.

He soon learnt the business from Mr Fitzwarren, married his daughter Alice, and in time became the Lord Mayor of London three times, just as the bells had said.

The real Richard Whittington was the son of a knight and himself a rich merchant in London. He served three terms as Lord Mayor of London: 1397–99, 1406–07, and 1419–20.

He died in 1423.

*

Florence Nightingale

FLORENCE NIGHTINGALE, named after the Italian city where she was born, was a Victorian English girl from a family whose parents expected her to follow the accepted path for girls of her upbringing, to marry well, have a family and be a lady of leisure. So when, as a young woman, she announced that she wanted to become a nurse they were very much against it. At that time girls from her background rarely, if ever, had jobs and in any case nursing was not considered in the least suitable.

Florence was obviously a determined character, because she turned down a proposal of marriage, and finally persuaded her parents to allow her to take up nursing in 1853, when she was 33. She is most famous for the team of nurses she assembled during the Crimean War at the request of Sidney Herbert, the Minister for War, a family friend who recognised and respected her abilities. She took them with her to be the first female nurses in the military hospitals of Turkey. She became extremely popular in England for her nursing work with the army and was known as 'the Lady with the lamp' because she carried a lamp around the wards when she visited her wounded soldier-patients at night. There are well known portraits of her, dressed in her Victorian crinoline and carrying her lamp.

The pictures warmed the hearts of the public and a great deal of money was collected in her name. She used the money to improve nursing care in England, by setting up training schools and making it a respectable profession for women. After her return from the Crimea she retired from public attention and spent the remainder of her long life encouraging and helping nurses and the nursing profession.

Enthusiasts might like to visit the Florence Nightingale Museum, St Thomas' Hospital, 2 Lambeth Palace Road, London, SE1 7EW www.florence-night-ingale.co.uk

*

Nelson at Trafalgar

'England expects that every man will do his duty.'

WITH THESE WORDS Horatio Nelson inspired his squadron be-fore the Battle of Trafalgar, in 1805, during which he died. At his death, Britain lost and mourned a great leader who longed for honour and glory but was kind and compassionate to the sailors he commanded.

He was born in Norfolk, to a large family and joined the Navy at the age of 12. He became a captain at 20, and fought many battles in one of which he lost the sight in his right eye; in another he lost his right arm. As a commander he was known for bold action, and the occasional disregard of orders from his seniors. He won the Battle of Copenhagen when he ignored orders to cease action by putting his telescope to his blind eye and claimed he couldn't see the signal to stop attacking.

Nelson became Vice-Admiral and, under his leadership, the British Navy proved its supremacy over the French. His most famous battle, at Cape Trafalgar, saved Britain from the threat of invasion by Napoleon, but it was to be his last.

At about 1.15 pm on 21 October 1805, when the battle was at its height, Nelson was on the quarterdeck of his flagship, HMS *Victory*, with his friend Captain Thomas Hardy, when he was shot by a French musketman. Nelson was carried to the ship's cockpit, below the waterline, where the wounded could be treated out of the line of fire.

'You can do nothing for me,' he said to the surgeon who bent anxiously over him; 'I have but a short time to live.'

He was right: 'Pray for me, doctor,' whispered Nelson while the battle raged above. At every cheer that told of victory, a smile passed over the face of the dying man. At last the news came down, that the enemy was all but defeated, and hope was expressed that Nelson would live to bring the good news home to England.

He longed to see his friend, Captain Hardy, who was busy on deck. At last Hardy managed to snatch a few moments to visit his dying friend. Nelson grasped his hand.

'Well, Hardy, how goes the battle? How goes the day with us?' he cried.

'Very well, my lord,' was the reply; 'we have got 12 or 14 of the enemy's ships in our possession.'

'I am a dead man, Hardy,' he said presently. 'I am going fast; it will soon be all over with me.'

Hardy bent over his dying friend, then grasped him by the hand, and hurried back to his post on the deck feeling very sad.

'One would like to live a little longer,' Nelson said to the doctor when Hardy had gone.

'My lord,' was the heart-broken answer, 'unhappily for our country, nothing can be done for you.' And he turned away to hide his sorrow.

Another hour passed. At four o'clock Hardy returned. Grasping

Nelson's hand, he told him that the victory was almost complete. Some 15 ships had been taken.

'That is well,' said Nelson; 'but I had bargained for 20.'

Then, as he planned out the end of the battle, he imagined a rising gale, and the battered British fleet drifting ashore.

'Anchor, Hardy, anchor,' he said.

'I suppose, my lord, Admiral Collingwood will now take upon himself the direction of affairs,' said Hardy.

'Not while I live, Hardy, I hope,' cried Nelson, struggling to raise himself in bed. 'No; do you anchor, Hardy?'

'Shall we make the signal, sir?'

'Yes; for if I live I'll anchor,' was the firm reply.

These were his last commands.

'Kiss me, Hardy,' he whispered presently.

Reverently the captain knelt and kissed his cheek.

'Now I am satisfied,' murmured Nelson. 'Thank God, I have done my duty.'

Hardy had risen. He now stood looking silently at the dying Admiral. Suddenly he knelt down and kissed him again.

'Who is that?' asked Nelson.

'It is Hardy,' answered his friend.

'God bless you, Hardy,' murmured the dying man.

About half-past four – three hours after his wound – Nelson died. Before sunset all firing had ceased. The battle of Trafalgar was over.

The news of the two events was received in England with mingled joy and sorrow; 'God gave us the victory – but Nelson died.'

Noah's Ark

ONCE, LONG AGO, there lived a man called Noah, who had three sons – Shem, Ham, and Japheth. Noah and his family were good people, they believed in God and followed his wishes. However, they lived in a time when many people on the earth were very bad. And God became angry with the people, and decided to do something to wipe away all the wickedness.

God resolved that there would be a big flood, which would kill every living thing on earth – everyone except Noah and his family. God told him to build a big boat, called an ark – a boat big enough to hold Noah and his wife and their three sons Shem, Ham, and Japheth and also their wives. Then God told Noah to bring into the ark two of all living creatures, male and female, along with every kind of food to be stored to sustain the animals and his family while on the ark.

Noah obeyed everything God commanded him to do. And, after they entered the ark, God sent a great rain that lasted for forty days and forty nights. It rained and it rained, and the water rose higher and higher till you could not see even the tallest mountain. The waters flooded the earth and every living thing on the face of the earth was wiped out.

At last, as the waters began to recede, the ark came to rest on the mountains of Ararat. Noah and his family continued to wait for many months while the surface of the earth dried out.

Finally, one day Noah sent out a dove to search for a place to rest. The dove came back having found no place to land. After seven days, Noah again sent out the dove and this time the bird returned with an olive branch in its beak.

It was time. Noah lifted the covering off the ark and saw dry ground before him. And he and his wife and his three sons Shem, Ham, and Japheth and their wives and all the animals went out of the ark to start life on land again.

The first thing Noah did was to build an altar, and to make offerings of some of the animals to God. God saw this and was pleased, and he sent a rainbow as a sign that he would never again send a flood to kill all the people.

*

Demeter and Persephone

PERSEPHONE WAS THE beautiful young daughter of the goddess Demeter and Zeus, the king of the gods. She lived a peaceful, happy life away from the other gods. One day, while she was picking flowers with some nymphs, Hades, the king of the underworld, burst out through the surface of the earth and snatched her. He dragged her into the underworld, against her will, to be his wife.

Her mother, Demeter, searched high and low for her, becoming increasingly worried and miserable. As well as being Persephone's mother, Demeter was goddess of the Earth and made sure that the crops grew, the flowers blossomed, and fruit appeared on the trees.

But while she fretted for her daughter, she did not tend to her business, and the people on the earth began to suffer – there was no food to eat, and the earth became a gloomy and barren place. Finally, Zeus, hearing the cries of the hungry people and urged by the other gods who saw how they suffered, went down in to the Underworld and forced Hades to return Persephone to her mother. But Hades had tricked Persephone into eating six pomegranate seeds – and once you have dined in the Underworld, there can be no going back…

So a deal was struck – Persephone was allowed to return to her mother, but for each of the pomegranate seeds she had eaten, she must spend a month of the year with Hades as his bride in the gloomy Underworld, the realm of the dead.

For each of the six months that Persephone returned to the earth with her mother, the land blossomed and flourished – but for the other six, when she was forced down to the darkness below, her mother mourned, and the crops didn't grow… And so we have our warm, fruit and flower-filled summer months, and our hard winter months when the trees are bare, and the ground is cold.

✳

Alexander and Bucephalus

ALEXANDER THE GREAT was exceptional among most soldiers of his time in his devotion to his horse, Bucephalus. The horse's name means 'Ox Head', which he was called because he had a beautifully wide and handsome forehead.

Alexander's father, Philip, had paid a great sum of money for Bucephalus, but he found the horse vicious and unmanageable. He was about to have the horse destroyed when Alexander, then aged 12, asked if he might try to ride him. Despite his father's scorn, and doubtless a lot of sniggering from the stable boys, Alexander walked quietly up to Bucephalus, stroked him, swung his head towards the sun and mounted him with ease. He was the only person to realise that the horse had been terrified by his own prancing shadow. His father was delighted, and gave the horse to Alexander, who was the only person Bucephalus ever allowed to ride him.

Bucephalus was Alexander's faithful warhorse through all his triumphant campaigns for many years. At the Battle of Hydaspes in 326, when Alexander defeated the King of India, Bucephalus, by then very old, was wounded in the neck and side. But in spite of his terrible wounds he carried Alexander to safety before he collapsed and died. Alexander was grief stricken and had Bucephalus buried with full military honours and a city built over his grave.

◆6◆
Get with It Granny

What on earth are they talking about?

As soon as your grandchildren start at primary school, they are out in a world of which you probably know little, and will come home with a new and mystifying vocabulary. This gets worse as they get older – some teenagers are so incomprehensible they might be speaking Japanese for all you know. What, for example, does Bebo, Emo or Wifi mean? What are Heelys? If you can do two out of those four, you're already a with it, Granny – cool!

But most of us need a little help, and there's no one better placed to give it than your grandchildren themselves. They'll probably enjoy explaining, in a pitying tone. They are certainly the best people to call on for help with mobile phones and computers – they seem to have an intuitive understanding of modern technology. Remember how they taught you to use the video recorder and how to play a DVD?

One thing is for sure, being able to use a computer is a central part of modern life, and oldies who have held out against it are beginning to feel isolated.

Computer literacy opens up a whole new world, in which all kinds of information is (literally) at your fingertips, you can communicate with strangers world-wide, and shop for everything under the sun.

Don't worry – mastering the basics of a computer is surprisingly painless. One of the best ways to learn is to attend classes at your local library. These are generally free. If you need one-to-one help and can afford it, hire your own geek (see *Teenspeak*, below) to give you home tuition. Sharing a teacher with a friend will halve the cost and be more fun.

If you'd rather teach yourself, with a bit of help from your grandchildren, the basics for PC users are explained in an excellent book, *Computing for Seniors in Easy Steps,* by Sue Price, and for Mac users there is a similar book, *Mac Computing for Seniors in Easy Steps*, by Nick Vandome.

Once you are comfortable with using the computer, there are several websites designed for the grandparent generation, including www.silversurfersseventy.co.uk and www.goodgranny.com. You may also want to get a digital camera, so you can download your photographs for distribution by email to faraway family members. Go to the website www.wikihow.com and type 'Digital photos' in the Search box to get step-by-step instructions on how to save photos from your digital camera onto your PC.

You can learn to edit them, making them look really classy and, if you invest in a special printer, print them on glossy photographic paper. Every Christmas our son-in-law uses his computer to make a wonderful calendar of family photographs for each month.

Remember that computers need to be monitored when children are around. If your grandchildren are coming to stay, you might want to block them from accessing certain sites – there are several downloadable packages, which will allow you to filter what Internet contents reach you. The best thing to do is go to a large computer shop such as PC World or John Lewis, and discuss it with them.

Granny's Technical Glossary

Apple – as in, 'my Apple-Mac has crashed', is the most popular brand of computer for the design-conscious person. If you are thinking of getting one, be aware that the computer and related gadgets operate in a completely different way to any other brand.

Bebo – a social networking website similar to Facebook (see *below*). Popular with younger users than the Facebook crowd, it's used by children as young as ten and upwards.

Blackberry – your grandchildren are unlikely to have one, but your sons/daughters might not be able to tear themselves away from theirs: a tiny, portable computer and phone, on which they can check their emails and hence be in touch with their office 24 hours a day.

Blog – an online diary, which can be viewed by anyone on the Internet. Some have been so interesting they have been turned into very successful books.

Chat room – a virtual (see *below*) discussion forum, a place on the Internet where people with similar interests can communicate by typing messages on their computer. NB. Don't let your grand-children go onto one: people can enter an unmoderated chat room (again, see *below*) without any verification of who they are and may have sinister motives.

Downloading – the term used to describe the process of moving computer data from one location to another. Although the term is normally used to describe the transfer, or downloading, of data from the Internet, it is also used to describe the transfer of photos from a camera memory card to the computer, as in 'I downloaded photos on to my PC.'

Email – writing and receiving correspondence on the Internet, via computer. It can be faster and cheaper than the telephone.

Ebook – an electronic version of a print book that can be read using a computer or an ebook reader. Ebook readers have been slow to take off, partly because – unlike the i-pod or MP3 Players – the early models were unappealing.

Facebook – a social networking website where a network of friends communicate. It's mainly, though by no means exclusively, used by students and younger people. It can become almost addictive and has been banned in some offices for wasting employees working time. Users can add friends and send them messages, post photos and update their personal profile to tell friends about themselves.

Google – now a term so commonly used that it has become a verb, as in 'to Google'. Google is a giant search engine via which you can find out pretty much anything you could ever want to know. You type a word or phrase in the search box and it comes up with thousands of references from which you pick the relevant one.

Hacker – a person who gains access to computer programmes by breaking through or evading their protection system. The process is called hacking.

Homepage – your homepage is what appears automatically on your screen when you connect to the Internet. You can choose your own homepage. It may be something personal like a photograph of your grandchildren, or a site you use every day such as the weather forecast.

I-pod – a digital music player designed by Apple on which you can store music and listen to it – a much neater, more efficient version of an old Sony Walkman. The i-pod was the first version of this item, though Apple continue to refine the design and features, and there are also 'mini i-pods', 'i-pod nanos' and 'shuffles' (these last make quite a good present for younger children; they are smaller, cheaper gadgets on which you can store a manageable number of songs/stories, to be listened to at random). Older grandchildren may talk about 'down-loading' songs/music, which means transferring the music onto the i-pod via a computer – white earphones and wires and a faraway expression are the tell-tell sign of this machine.

Internet – a worldwide system of interconnected computer networks embracing millions of smaller domestic, academic, business, and government networks, which together carry various information and services, such as email, online chat, websites and other resources of the World Wide Web (WWW).

MP3 player – like an i-pod, this is a digital music player which allows you to download songs (and, increasingly, books...) to store and listen to.

MSN messenger – a popular instant messaging programme created by the MicroSoft computer network. Children as young as six or seven are likely to have a messaging address, and ask to go on the computer to 'chat' to their friends. It is like 'texting' but on the computer screen rather than on the phone.

Nintendo DS – a hand held computer and games console, much desired by children of ten and upwards.

Nintendo Wii – is the most recent 'games console', which really means a super high-tech computer that enables children to play with other children all over the world, and to play virtual games – it is also used by grown ups, and you can even keep fit with it.

Online – when you connect your computer to the Internet to send or receive email or to look at a website, it's known as 'going online'.

Parental Control – a feature that allows parents – or grandparents! – to 'lock' website and Internet programs that they consider unsuitable for children. A 'locked' channel or program can only be 'unlocked' with the special parental access code.

PC – a personal computer, which can be either a desktop, or a portable laptop, and is basically any brand of computer that is not an Applemac (or 'Mac')…

Search engine – a directory on the Internet, which can list websites at which you are likely to find information. Popular engines include Google, Yahoo and Snap.

Skype – a computer software program enabling you to make telephone calls over the Internet to other Skype users free of charge. The program is easy to download from the Internet (see *Downloading*) – and offers an excellent way of keeping in touch with friends and family abroad without having to pay extortionate phone bills.

Tecchie – what you will be when you've mastered the technical side of computing.

Texting – the sending of a written message from one mobile phone to another. 'Texting' is now a fundamental part of any mobile phone user's life, not least because it is cheaper than actual voice messages. Pretty well anyone over seven can text.

There are, confusingly, various different formats that you can write your message in. The most commonly used is 'Predictive Text', an input technology that predicts the word you are typing, reducing the number of keystrokes that you need to make, ie it allows words to be entered by a single keypress for each letter, as opposed to the multiple keypress approach used in the older generation of phones. Refer to your mobile phone's user manual to find out how you can turn this feature off and on.

Text language usually consists of abbreviations and short cuts to save time when typing a message. It also generally involves not using the 5 vowels, A, E, I, O and U. For example, YR = YouR...but it can also include acronyms where the first letter of a word is used, like BFN = Bye For Now.

Single letters can replace words. For instance:

• be becomes b
• see becomes c
• are becomes r
• you becomes u

Among younger phone users, this has developed into a language of its own.

C U L8R – see you later
WOT R U UP 2 – what are you up to/what are you doing?
2MORO – tomorrow
G8 – great
2NITE – tonight
ALOL – Actually laughing out loud
CSL – Can't stop laughing
DIKU – Do I know you?

HAK – Hugs and kisses
JK – Just kidding
KEWL – Cool
AYK – As you know
ILU – I love you
B4 – Before
BW – Best wishes
BTW – by the way
OMG – oh my god
THNX – thanks

Virtual – an imaginary version of something real. The term takes on many uses in the computer world as a wide variety of devices and software exist for the sole purpose of providing simulations of reality. For example, many feel that the Internet is a virtual world unto itself.

Virtual reality – this is a realistic environment often used for entertainment, which uses three-dimensional images, stereo sound, and tactile stimulation to give the user a feeling of actually living through a physical experience.

WWW – the World Wide Web (See *Internet,* above). Website addresses are prefaced with www.

Website – a collection of web 'pages' giving written information, images or videos, accessible via the Internet. A website may be commercial (information about products, often including mail order facilities), public information (government agencies etc.) general information (wikipedia), or personal. Together they make up the World Wide Web and can be accessed from the homepage of your computer.

Wifi – Short for 'Wireless Fidelity', this is a radio frequency standard used to connect devices, such as computers, using a wireless connection; instead of computers being connected with cables, signals are sent over radio frequencies. The idea of having no wires around the place is tempting, but I would suggest you need a computer doctor to set this up!

Wikipedia – a giant online encyclopaedia of pretty much anything you can think of; it is edited by the users, so not 100% reliable. Covers everything from the biography of Cary Grant to the history of coal mining – useful for helping grandchildren with their homework.

YouTube – a hugely successful video sharing website, where users can upload, view and share video clips.

Toys and Crazes

We all know who Thomas and Barbie are, and we know how to play Monopoly, but who is Princess Mariposa and what are scoubidous?

Playground crazes come and go, and some seem to loop back repeatedly. With us, it was hopscotch one term, skipping the next, then clapping games, then yoyos. Jacks came and went, and came back. All these are revived from time to time. Collecting and swapping is always popular (remember cigarette cards?).

Just now primary school children love *Dr Who* toys and Ben 10's 'alien heroes', *Ben 10* being an American cartoon. *Star Wars* is making new fans, and figures and weapons are being collected.

Many of these can be bought secondhand, on websites such as Amazon, and canny older children use 'swap' websites to trade their cars, toys, figures and games (swapitshop.com is one of the leading, safe websites of this type).

Here are some current favourites:

Bratz – these dolls are very popular with young girls, and they are characterised by big heads with rather small bodies – there is now a film that goes with the dolls!

Crocs – as well as must-have toys, there are must-have clothes. Crocs are chunky rubber beach shoes, often in day-glow colours. And now there are Croc wellies and pumps.

Heelys – trainers with a wheel in the heel, which enable the wearer to roll along the ground, rather than walk. Much coveted by children. (Grannies should not, under any circumstances, be tempted to invest in a pair and join their grandchildren for a heely session in the park:

the wheel being located in the heel rather than the toe of the shoe is somehow completely counterintuitive, and unwary users will most likely find themselves falling hard on their bottoms.

High School Musical: Disney's made-for-TV film broke all viewing records in America and has become a huge craze, spawning lunchboxes, bags, umbrellas and duvet covers.

Light-up shoes – shoes for young children with flashing lights, rather like bicycle lights, set into the back of the heel. Can be useful for keeping an eye on your grandchild in a crowd – unless all the others are wearing them too.

Match Attax – football trading cards, hugely popular with boys.

Scoubidous – colourful, supple, hollow plastic tubes usually about 80cm long. They are plaited and knotted to make friendship bracelets, key chains, and other trinkets. I remember them being all the rage in the late 1950s, though I don't think they were called Scoubidous then, they are now enjoying a revival.

Sleepovers – staying the night with your best friend(s) or having them to stay with you. A fashion is developing for super sophisticated (and expensive) sleepovers. A night at Kew Gardens, or a night in front of the giant aquarium in Hull are both offered as exciting sleepovers. (See *Great Days Out*)

Teenspeak

Awesome – great!

Bare – a lot of, very.

Book – cool (comes from the first option given by predictive text when trying to type c-o-o-l).

Canes – as in 'that really canes', means 'that really hurts'.

Cool – means anything from 'great' to 'fine' to 'no problem', the particular usage can probably be gauged by the tone used by your grandchild.

Cotch – to hang out, relax, or sleep at someone's house (possibly derived from the French 'se coucher', meaning to lie down).

Deep – horrible, not nice.

Dork, geek, nerd – swot.

Dry – dull, boring, stupid, unfunny (as in a bad joke).

Emo – a term meaning 'emotionally unstable', used to describe a moody, volatile person as in 'he/she's a total emo'. It is linked to a gloomy, sometimes suicidal style of music. Emos tend to wear black.

Extra – over the top, wild, crazy, as in 'That girl is totally extra...'

Jokes – funny, enjoyable, as in 'that party was jokes'.

Legend – as in 'he's a legend', means 'he's pretty great'.

Mint – cool, great.

Random – as in 'that's quite random', means 'that's a bit unusual/ unexpected/that came from nowhere'.

Rinsed – made a fool of, shown, dressed down, as in 'he got completely rinsed by those big boys'.

Sad – pitifully bad or stupid, as in 'the way he danced was really sad'.

Safe – good, cool, sweet.

Sick – good, cool, as in 'that's sick', 'that sounds interesting, cool'.

Skater – Someone who hangs about with a skateboard all the time, and dresses in skateboarding clothes.

Skeen – great! cool!

So fun – an emphatic, as in 'it was *so* fun'.

Vexed – irritated, angry (an old word, back in fashion).

Whatever – the verbal equivalent of a shrug, as in 'So what', or 'I couldn't care less'.

Wicked! – great!

♥ 7 ♥

Who's Who – Things You Haven't Really Forgotten

THIS CHAPTER CONSISTS mostly of lists, giving the sort of information which may come in handy to answer grandchildren's questions, to help them with homework and school projects, or simply because it's interesting or quirky or amusing. I've also listed some classic books and films that you and your grandchildren will both enjoy reading and watching together. One of the pleasures for grandparents is introducing the children to their own beloved stories and movies, and sharing their interests.

Kings and Queens of England

As an additional aide memoire for granny, and to find out what the kings and queens did, I recommend *Our Island Story* – I still have a well-used copy from my childhood and often refer to it if I need to know dates and events in history.

Children who already know a little bit of history will chortle at *1066 and All That*.

Alfred The Great	*871 - 899*
Canute	*1016 - 1035*
Harold II	*1066 -1066*
William the Conqueror	*1066 -1087*
William Rufus	*1087 -1100*
Henry I	*1100 - 1135*
Stephen	*1135 - 1154*
Henry II	*1154 -1189*
Richard 1	*1189 -1199*
John	*1199 - 1216*
Henry III	*1216 - 1272*
Edward 1	*1272 - 1307*
Edward II	*1307 - 1327*
Edward III	*1327 - 1377*
Richard II	*1377 - 1399*
Henry IV	*1399 - 1413*
Henry V	*1413 - 1422*
Henry VI	*1422 - 1461*
Edward IV	*1461 - 1483*
Edward V	*1483*
Richard III	*1483 - 1485*
Henry VII	*1485 - 1509*
Henry VIII	*1509 - 1547*
Edward VI	*1547 - 1553*
Mary Tudor	*1553 - 1558*
Elizabeth	*1558 - 1603*
James I	*1603 - 1625*
Charles I	*1625 - 1649*
Commonwealth and Protectorate	*1649 — 1660*
Charles II	*1660 - 1685*
James II	*1685 - 1688*
William of Orange and Mary, jointly	*1689 - 1694*
William III sole ruler	*1694 - 1702*
Anne	*1702 - 1714*
George I	*1714 - 1727*
George II	*1727 - 1760*
George III	*1760 - 1820*
George IV	*1820 - 1830*
William IV	*1830 - 1837*
Victoria	*1837 - 1901*
Edward VII	*1901 - 1910*
George V	*1910 - 1936*
Edward VIII	*1936*
George V1	*1936 - 1952*
Elizabeth II	*1952 -*

Willie, Willie, Harry, Stee,
Harry, Dick, John, Harry III
One-two-three Neds, Richard two,
Harrys four, five, six....then who ?
Edwards four, five, Dick the Bad,
Harrys (twain), Ned Six (the lad)
Mary, Bessie, James you ken
Then Charlie, Charlie, James again
Will and Mary, Anne of Gloria,
Georges four, Will four, Victoria
Edward VII next and then
Came George the Fifth in 1910
Ned the eighth soon abdicated
So George the Sixth was coronated
Then number two Elizabeth
And that's all folks (until her death)

Greek and Roman Gods

Greek Name	Roman Name	Title	Emblem
Zeus	Jupiter	King of the gods	thunderbolt/eagle
Hera	Juno	Queen of the gods	sceptre/diadem
Apollo	Phoebus Apollo	God of light	bow/lyre/ laurel wreath
Hermes	Mercury	Messenger of the gods	winged boots
Poseidon	Neptune	God of the sea	trident & chariot drawn by tritons: half men half fish
Ares	Mars	God of war	spear
Hephaistos	Vulcan	God of fire	blacksmith axe or hammer & anvil
Dionysus	Bacchus	God of wine	vine/ivy
Pan	Pan	God of woods & pastures	pipes
Eros	Cupid	God of love	bow & arrow
Hades	Pluto	God of the underworld	cockerel/dog/ sceptre
Athena	Minerva	Goddess of wisdom	owl/olive tree
Artemis	Diana	Goddess of the hunt & moon	hunter's bow
Aphrodite	Venus	Goddess of love/beauty	sceptre/myrtle /a dove
Demeter	Ceres	Goddess of fertility & harvest	lighted torch or sheaf of corn

Heroes and Creatures of Greek Myths and Legends

Heracles was the mightiest mortal. He was the son of the god Zeus. He was given 12 labours or tasks to complete as a test.

Perseus was also a son of Zeus. He slew the Medusa, a fearful monster or Gorgon, who turned people to stone.

Jason led the Argonauts in search of the Golden Fleece.

Theseus was King of Athens, the most important city in Greece. He killed the Minotaur, which was half-human, half-bull and lived in the labyrinth on the island of Crete.

Cyclops was a one-eyed monster, outwitted by Odysseus.

Pegasus was a winged horse and Bellerophon was the mortal who rode him.

Pandora was the first woman. She was responsible for letting evil into the world when she opened a forbidden box that was full of evil. Luckily one thing was left in the box: hope.

Atlas was a giant who supported the earth on his shoulders.

Narcissus was a beautiful young boy who gazed at his own reflection in a pool of water, fell in love with himself and wasted away as he gazed at his reflection until all that was left of him was a white flower – a narcissus.

The Titans were giants who ruled earth before the time of the Gods.

Midas was the richest human, a king who turned everything he touched into gold.

Many of the **Roman Gods** *are similar to the Greek gods, although they had some of their own:*

Janus, the god of creation, who stands at the gate of the year and looks both ways. That's why the first month is called January.

Lares and **Penates**, the household gods. The Penates were the gods of the larder and were prayed to and offered food at meals.

Flora was the goddess of spring.

Romulus and **Remus** were the twin sons of Mars, God of War. According to legend, they were abandoned at birth on the banks of the river Tiber and reared by a wolf. They were the founders of Rome and Romulus, who killed his brother, was the founder and first king of Rome, which was named after him.

Hindu Gods and Goddesses

The three main Gods are:

Brahma – the creator of the universe and the God of wisdom.

Shiva – the destroyer, often portrayed as dancing.

Vishnu – the sustainer and protector of the universe. He and his wife, Lakshmi, are often portrayed riding a huge eagle called Garude.

There are many other gods worshipped with offerings of flowers and food in Hindu temples and shrines. Some of the more important are:

Rama – he is worshipped as the example of how people should ideally be. He is brave, handsome, loyal and kind. His wife is the goddess, Sita.

Hanuman – the monkey God and the faithful servant of Rama.

Lakshmi – goddess of beauty and prosperity.

Krishna – one of the most popular gods and the god of love.

Ganesha – the elephant-headed god who brings knowledge and removes obstacles.

*

The Story of Shiva and Parvati

ONCE, THE GOD Shiva was called away from his home for a long time. His wife, the goddess Parvati, became so lonely without him that she made herself a little child out of clay mixed with her spit. Then, because she was a goddess, she breathed on the figure and brought it to life. She was very happy with the little boy she had created and was less lonely without her husband, Shiva.

When she went to the river to bathe one day, she left her little son behind and warned him not to let anyone enter her house while she was out. But that was the very day Shiva returned home. When he tried to enter his house, Parvati's son obeyed his mother's orders and barred the door, refusing to let Shiva in, no matter how much he ranted and raved. Finally Shiva became so angry that he cut off the child's head.

When Parvati arrived back and saw what Shiva had done she was mad with grief. She told Shiva that the boy, whose head he had chopped off, was their own child. Shiva was shocked and remorseful and promised to use his powers to bring him back to life. He ordered his servants to go out and to bring back the head of the first creature they came across. The first creature they met was a baby elephant and they immediately cut off its head and took it to the god. Shiva then used his powers to join the head of the baby elephant to the body of his dead son and brought him back to life as the elephant-headed god, Ganesha.

Norse Gods and Goddesses

Norse Gods and Goddesses were not immortal like the Greek and Roman Gods and could die or be killed in battle like humans.

Odin – the father of the Gods and God of War.

Balder – beloved son of Odin and a wise and gentle god.

Thor – patron of farmers and the god of thunder and lightning, but good thunder and lightning, which helped the crops to grow. The Norse believed that during a thunderstorm, Thor rode through the heavens on his chariot pulled by two goats, Tanngrisni ('gap-tooth') and Tanngnost ('tooth grinder'). Lightning flashed whenever he threw his hammer. There is a very silly poem about Thor:

> *Thor the God of thunder went riding on his filly*
> *I'm Thor, he cried*
> *The horse replied*
> *You forgot your thaddle, thilly!*

Frey – the God of peace and fertility and the patron God of horses.

Freya – goddess of love and beauty. She could disguise herself as a falcon and drove around in a carriage drawn by two cats.

Frigg – the wife of Odin and goddess of the home.

Loki – the trickster and shape-changer, a mischievous and malicious god.

Moon – guides the moon on its course.

Christian Saints and Their Martyrs

PATRON SAINTS

England: St George who slew a dragon to rescue a princess. His picture always shows him dressed as a knight and fighting the dragon with his lance. April 23

Ireland: St Patrick who brought Christianity to Ireland. He is supposed to have explained the Father, Son and Holy Ghost as part of one trinity by using the three-leafed shamrock as an example. There is a legend that he drove all the snakes out of Ireland and that's why there are none there today. March 17

Scotland: St Andrew, one of the apostles of Christ and a martyr whose symbol is an X as he was crucified upside down on an x-shaped cross. November 30

Wales: St David. The symbol of Wales, which is worn on his feast day, is the leek. St David was supposed to have lived on a diet of bread, water, watercress and leeks. March 1

OTHER SAINTS

St Catherine of Alexandria was martyred on a spiked wheel for refusing to marry the Emperor. Her symbol is the wheel. The firework, known as the Catherine Wheel, is said to be named after her. In France on her feast day, November 25th, girls over the age of 25 who were unmarried would wear the St Catherine's bonnet.

St Christopher is the patron saint of travellers. He is said to have carried a small child across a dangerous river and found that the child grew so heavy that he could barely support him on his shoulders. When he reached the other side of the river the child revealed himself as Christ and told the saint that the weight he had borne was the weight of sin. He is usually pictured fording a stream with a staff in his hand and a child on his back.

St Francis of Assisi is the patron saint of animals and is often pictured feeding birds. He was a rich and wild young man who changed his ways, gave away his riches and became extremely holy.

St Lucy was a young Christian girl who lived in Sicily in the fourth century. She did not wish to marry her suitor who was in love with her blue eyes, so she gouged them out – which seems a little extreme but they grew back again, twice as beautiful. Her suitor killed her and she was eventually made a saint. Her feast day, December 13th, is a national holiday in Sweden. Young girls dress in white and wear candle headdresses and boys wear pointed hats with stars on them. Mid-December is when the days are shortest so St Lucy's festival provides some fun at the bleakest time of year.

St Nicholas of Myra in Lycia (now Turkey) was a Bishop in the fourth century and the original Santa Claus. There is a story that he miraculously brought back to life three young boys who had been killed and pickled in a barrel by a mad butcher. He is also supposed to have been very generous and once, anonymously, threw three purses of coins into the home of a poor family who needed the money to provide dowries for three daughters.

This is why in the Netherlands, for example, secret presents are given in Dutch families on the eve of the feast of St Nicholas –

December 6th, the feast of Sinter Klaus.

St Thomas Becket was Archbishop of Canterbury and Chancellor of England in the thirteenth century. He disagreed with King Henry II on some important matters. Henry is said to have exclaimed, 'Who will rid me of this turbulent priest,' and four of Henry's knights rushed to Canterbury Cathedral where Thomas Becket had taken shelter, and murdered him.

St Martin of Tours was a Roman soldier in the fourth century who is supposed to have cut his military cloak in two to give half to a beggar – wonderfully portrayed in a painting by El Greco – and later dreamt that the beggar was Christ. He became a Christian and eventually a saint. November 11th

OTHER SAINTS WHO ARE PRAYED TO FOR SPECIAL HELP:

St Jude, patron saint of lost causes. He seems to have brought it off for some people as advertisements used to appear in the Personal Column of *The Times* newspaper offering 'thanks to the Blessed Saint Jude for favours received'.

St Blaise to cure sore throats. February 3

St Anthony of Padua to find lost things. June 13

St Cecilia is the patron saint of musicians. November 2

The Night Sky

THE MOON

The first flight to land on the moon was on July 20, 1969 when American astronaut, Neil Armstrong, left the Apollo 11 space craft and walked on the moon, describing it as a small step for man but 'One giant leap for mankind'.

You can watch the moon change shape each month. This is called the phases of the moon. The phases happen as the sun lights up different parts of the moon. The moon takes $29{1/2}$ days to complete its phases, changing gradually from being a New Moon until, as the sun lights up more and more of the moon's surface, it finally becomes a Full Moon.

When the moon is growing smaller it is described as 'waning'; when it is getting bigger and brighter it is 'waxing'.

THE PLANETS

They move in a circle around the sun. There are eight planets in the solar system, all kept in place by the huge power of the sun (its gravitational pull). They are mostly named after Greek gods:

Venus the brightest planet is often mistaken for a UFO and is also called the Evening Star.

Mars is known for its reddish colour.

Jupiter is the second brightest planet.

Saturn takes over 29 years to orbit the sun. It's the planet with rings around it.

Mercury is the nearest planet to the sun.

Uranus and **Neptune** are much further away and can't really be seen except by scientists with special equipment. And of course, **Earth** is the only planet able to support life. Unlike Saturn, it takes only 365 days to orbit the sun.

Jupiter is the biggest planet. Earth is fifth largest.

Pluto used to be the smallest planet but it was downgraded in 2006 and is no longer officially considered to be a planet. It is now known as a dwarf planet. An unmanned spacecraft is currently on its way to explore Pluto and is expected to reach it by 2015.

At different times five of the planets can be seen. Three are easy to spot – Venus, Jupiter and Mars. Venus is by far the brightest and can be seen in the east or west at sunrise and sunset.

THE STARS

On a clear cloudless night, particularly in the country where there is less light pollution, stargazing can be fun. Look out for constellations, which are groups of stars that appear to form a pattern in the sky when looked at by the naked eye or through a telescope. There are 88 known constellations named after the shapes they make in the sky, for example Leo the lion, Scorpio the scorpion, the swan Cygnus, and the bears, Ursa major and Ursa minor.

Stella Polaris, the Pole Star, is always in the North, almost directly above the North Pole. It is also the only star that doesn't appear to move through the sky. To find the North either use a compass or watch the evening sun, remembering that the sun always sets in the West. From there it should be simple to find North, East, South and West (a helpful mnemonic is Naughty Elephants Squirt Water) and so to find the North Star. Some of the easiest constellations to recognise are, The Plough – a group of stars that look like an old-fashioned plough or a saucepan and at the right time of year, between July and November, Cygnus, the swan, which can be seen high overhead in the night sky. Orion's Belt consists of three stars in a straight line.

Tales, Proverbs & Superstitions

★ An old superstition about magpies produced this rhyme:

One for sorrow,
two for joy,
three for a girl,
four for a boy,
five for silver,
six for gold,
seven for a secret that's never been told.

★ Another is that if only one magpie is seen you must spit on your finger and make a little cross on your shoe.

★ *Tinker, tailor, soldier, sailor, rich man, poor man, beggar man, thief...*
This game is played with plum stones when eating stewed plums or prunes or any other fruit with stones. You count the number of stones as you say this rhyme to see whom you will marry.

★ It's unlucky to see the new moon through glass.

★ Drinking water from the wrong side of the glass to stop hiccups. Some say it works some say it doesn't. If it works it's probably the act of bending your body over the glass. It never works if you try to tilt the glass towards you, you will end up spilling it down your front.

★ To get rid of warts, steal a bit of meat, rub the wart and bury the meat. As the meat rots the wart will disappear.

★ Eating up all your crusts will make your hair curl.

★ Carrots help you to see in the dark.

★ If a nettle stings you, find a dock leaf and rub it on the sting to make it better.

★ Don't make a face because if the wind changes you will be stuck with it.

ABOUT THE WEATHER...

★ *Red sky at night, shepherd's delight.*
  Red sky in the morning, shepherd's warning.

★ *March winds and April showers*
  Bring forth May flowers.

★ *Hurrah! Hurrah! The first of May, outdoor games begin today.*

★ *The North wind doth blow*
And we shall have snow
And what will poor robin do then, poor thing?
He'll sit in a barn
And keep himself warm
And hide his head under his wing.

★ *St Swithin's day if thou dost rain*
For forty days it will remain.
St Swithin's day if thou be fair
For forty days 'twill rain no more.

St Swithin's day is on July 15th and is in memory of a Saxon bishop of Winchester. When he died he was buried in one place but later his body was moved from its original burial place to a tomb in Winchester Cathedral. During the ceremony to celebrate his re-burial it rained and didn't stop for 40 days, hence the rhyme and superstition.

★ Many religions have light festivals and in cold northern climates they often take place in mid-winter, partly so that people can have a bit of jollity to get them through to spring, when it gets warmer. Candlemas Day, on February 2nd, when candles were blessed by the clergy (forty days after Christmas) is one of these. According to weather lore, if the sun comes out on this day there will be six more weeks of winter weather. February 2nd is also the day that hedgehogs are supposed to poke their snouts out from underground where they have been hibernating, to see if it is going to be less wintry. In

America, groundhogs are supposed to do the same:

If Candlemas day be dry and fair
The half of winter's to come and more
If Candlemas day be wet and foul
The half of winter's gone at yule.

★ If the cows are lying down, it's going to rain.

★ *Ne'er cast a clout*
  Til May is out.

This is definitely a warning not to start putting on summer clothes too soon. Whether it means you should wait until the end of the month of May or until hawthorn blossom is out in late April or early May, is not known.

★ *Rain before seven, sunshine before eleven.*

★ *Ash before oak, we'll have a soak,*
  Oak before ash, we'll get a splash.

★ If the bootlace seaweed you brought home from the beach at the end of the summer holidays gets damp and slimy, it's going to rain.

NANNY'S SAYINGS

★ Up the wooden stairs to Bedfordshire

★ We're not at home to Mr Tantrum

★ Leave some food on your plate for Mr Manners

★ Elbows off the table

★ Handsome is as handsome does

★ If you go on looking at yourself in that mirror it'll crack.

★ If you take the last morsel on the plate, you can have either a handsome husband or ten thousand a year.

★ Mark my words, there'll be tears before bedtime.

Golden Oldies

CLASSIC CHILDREN'S BOOKS AND STORIES

Ant and Bee and Kind Dog, by Angela Banner

The Story of Babar, by Jean de Brunhoff

Winnie the Pooh, by AAMilne and illustrated by EH Shephard

Where the Wild Things Are, by Maurice Sendak

The Cat in the Hat, by Dr Seuss

Charlotte's Web, by EB White

The Tale of Samuel Whiskers, and other stories by Beatrix Potter

Aesop's Fables (these can be bought as a book or downloaded free from the Internet and make good bedtime or any time stories - they are short).

The Fairy Tales of Hans Christian Andersen

Grimm's Fairy Tales

NB Some of these stories can be obtained in the Ladybird series. They are simply told, small children love them and you can find them in charity shops or buy them on the Internet.

The Little Grey Rabbit Books, by Alison Uttley

The Selfish Giant, by Oscar Wilde

Little Tim and the Brave Sea Captain, and others in the series, by Edward Ardizzone

The Happy Prince, by Oscar Wilde

The Cuckoo Clock and The Tapestry Room, by Mrs Molesworth

The Noddy books, by Enid Blyton

The Milly-Molly-Mandy Stories, by Joyce Lancaster Brisley

The Story of Little Black Sambo, by Helen Bannerman
The Pied Piper of Hamelin, by Robert Browning
Just So Stories and The Jungle Book, by Rudyard Kipling

For older children:
Peter Pan, by JM Barrie
Alice in Wonderland, by Lewis Carroll
The Water Babies, by Charles Kingsley
The Red Fairy Book, the Blue, Yellow, Olive, etc. Fairy Books, ed.
Andrew Laing
Treasure Island, by RL Stevenson
A Little Princess, by Frances Hodgson Burnett
The Secret Garden, by Frances Hodgson Burnett
Pippi Longstocking, by Astrid Lindgren
Charlie and the Chocolate Factory, by Roald Dahl
Tom's Midnight Garden, by Phillippa Pearce
The Silver Sword, by Ian Serrallier
The Sword in the Stone, by TH White
The Chronicles of Narnia, by CS Lewis
Swallows and Amazons, by Arthur Ransome
The Railway Children, by E Nesbit
Black Beauty, by Anna Sewell
National Velvet, by Enid Bagnold
The Family From One End Street, by Eve Garnett
Just William, by Richmal Crompton
Emil and the Detectives, by Eric Kastner
A Traveller in Time, by Alison Uttley
Brother Dusty Feet, by Rosemary Sutcliff

Around the World in Eighty Days, by Jules Verne
The Borrowers, by Mary Norton
Anne of Green Gables, by LM Montgomery
The Adventures of Asterix, by René Goscinny
Tintin, by Hergé
Mallory Towers, by Enid Blyton
Down with Skool and other Molesworth books, by Geoffrey Willans
and Ronald Searle.

CHILDREN'S FILMS

The British Board of Film Classification rates all children's films for suitability. U is considered suitable for children of four and over. All of the films listed below are U, unless marked PG, which means 'suitable for general viewing – although some scenes may be unsuitable for younger children'. 12A means children under 12 may see the film, at a cinema, if accompanied by an adult; children over 12 may see it unaccompanied by an adult. 13A is self-explanatory.

Some of these films are classics, perhaps older than some grannies. Others are yarns and adventures for children of all ages and some are more modern, usually involving sophisticated special effects or occasional double entendres, which generally go over the heads of younger audiences.

Disney:
Fantasia
Snow White and the Seven Dwarfs

Beauty and the Beast
Lady and the Tramp
101 Dalmations
Bambi
Jungle Book
Ratatouille (about a young French rat called Rémy)
Babe (about a pig raised by sheepdogs)
Finding Nemo (about a fish)
Toy Story 1 and 2
Free Willy (about an orca whale)
Wallace & Gromit in The Curse of the Were-Rabbit
Enchanted (a fairy tale princess in modern-day New York)

Musicals:
The Sound of Music
The King and I
My Fair Lady
Mary Poppins
Oliver
Chitty Chitty Bang Bang
Bedknobs and Broomsticks
Bugsy Malone (a gangster film where all the gangsters are children
and their guns are 'splurge guns' which cover people in cream)
Annie
The Wizard of Oz

Christmas classics:
Miracle on 34th Street (rated PG for some mild language)

Scrooge (with Alistair Sim, 1951; it's called *A Christmas Carol* in
America)
White Christmas
Polar Express
The Snowman

General:
Black Beauty (a good old weepie for granny)
Lassie (ditto)
The Incredible Journey (and another!)
National Velvet
The Secret Garden
The Railway Children
Charlie and The Chocolate Factory, PG
ET: The Extra-Terrestrial
The Neverending Story, PG
The Red Balloon (short and sweet 35 minutes long)
Around the World in Eighty Days (the original 1956 version is
the best)
The Muppet Movie
The Princess Diaries
Mon Oncle (Tati's first colour film, whose humour is probably
an acquired taste, but an absolute must for some)

For older children:
Oliver Twist (the original black and white 1948 film, directed by
David Lean, with Alec Guinness as Fagin)
The Star Wars Trilogy PG – for some sci-fi violence

Superman 1 and 2, PG

Home Alone, PG

The Chronicles of Narnia –The Lion, the Witch and the Wardrobe
(rated PG for the battle scenes and some frightening moments)

Danny Champion of the World

Raiders of the Lost Ark, PG

The Golden Compass, PG 13

The Harry Potter Films (all of which are rated PG, but can
be surprisingly violent and frightening, so not recommended
for sensitive under 9s)

Gandhi, PG

King Kong, PG (the 1933 original)

The Great Escape

Reach for the Sky

The Million Pound Note

The Winslow Boy

Record Breakers

Children, specially boys, love to know what and where is the tallest, smallest, oldest, fastest, most superlative anything in the whole wide world. Once a boy has learned to read, the *Guinness Book of Records* will keep him happy for hours. Here are a few examples:

The **tallest man** in medical history for whom there is irrefutable evidence is Robert Pershing Wadlow. He was from Illinois, in the USA. When he was last measured in 1940, he was found to be 2.72m (8ft 11.1in) tall. At the age of nine, he was able to carry his father, who was 1.8m (5 ft 11in) and weighed 77kg (170lb), up the stairs of the family home.

The world's **longest hair** belongs to Xie Qiuping (China) at 5.627m (18ft 5.54in) when measured on May 8, 2004. She has been growing her hair since 1973, from the age of 13.

The **deepest lake** in the world is Lake Baikal, 1,637m (5,371ft), deep. It's also the largest freshwater lake in the world by volume, holding approximately 20 per cent of the world's total surface fresh water.

The **fastest creatures** in the world are Peregrine falcons. They can fly horizontally at speeds up to 55mph, and, when flying in a downward dive to strike their prey, at over 270mph.

The **fastest land animal** is the cheetah. It can run at 70mph.

The **fastest running speed** of any human was achieved by Maurice Greene, with a sprint speed of 26.7mph. Compare that with the cheetah.

The **longest hiccup fit**: the world record was held by Charles Osborne of Iowa, starting in 1922. It lasted 68 years, ending mysteriously in 1990. He, hiccupped an estimated 430 million times. He died one year after his hiccups stopped.

The **highest mountain** in the world is Mount Everest, on the border between Nepal and China, in the Himalayas. The height of its summit above sea level is 8,848m or 29,029ft.

The **tallest building** on earth is The Taipei 101 Tower in Taiwan. Its height above ground is 509.2m. This includes the 60m spire; the building also holds the record for the highest roof (440m) and has the world's fastest lifts.

The **longest river** in the world is the Nile. It measures 6,695 kilometres from its source in Burundi, along the White Nile, to its delta on the Mediterranean Sea. Officially, the shortest river is the D River, Oregan, USA, which is just 37m long.

The **highest bridge** in the world is the Millau Viaduct in France. Its overall height is 336.4m.

The **largest of all fishes** is the Whale Shark, *Rhincodon typus*. Whale Sharks between 4 m to 12 m in length are often seen, but this species can reach a length of 18 m.

In case of difficulty in purchasing any Short Books title through normal channels, please contact BOOKPOST:
Tel 01624 836000
email bookshop@enterprise.net
www.bookpost.co.uk

Please quote ref. 'Short Books' i